7 Thoughts to Live Your Life By

A Guide to the Happy, Peaceful, & Meaningful Life

By I. C. Robledo

https://mentalmax.net/AMZbks

7 Thoughts to Live Your Life By: A Guide to the Happy, Peaceful, & Meaningful Life

Copyright © 2018 by Issac Robledo.

All Rights Reserved. No part of this book may be reproduced in any form without written permission from the author. Brief passages may be quoted for review purposes.

Disclaimer

Although the author and publisher have made every effort to ensure that the information in this book was correct at press time, the author and publisher do not assume and hereby disclaim any liability to any party for any loss, damage, or disruption caused by errors or omissions, whether such errors or omissions result from negligence, accident, or any other cause.

This book is not intended as a substitute for the medical advice of physicians. The reader should regularly consult a physician in matters relating to his/her health and particularly with respect to any symptoms that may require diagnosis or medical attention.

The views expressed are those of the author alone and should not be taken as expert instruction or commands. The reader is responsible for his or her own actions.

Adherence to all applicable laws and regulations, including international, federal, state, and local governing professional licensing, business practices, advertising, and all other aspects of doing business in the US, Canada, or any other jurisdiction is the sole responsibility of the purchaser or reader.

Neither the author nor the publisher assumes any responsibility or liability whatsoever on the behalf of the purchaser or reader of these materials.

Any perceived slight of any individual or organization is purely unintentional.

Table of Contents

An Introduction to the 7 Thoughts to Live Your Life By 1

Before You Continue 21

THOUGHT #1 : Focus on What You Can Control,
Not on What You Cannot Control 23

THOUGHT #2 : Focus on the Positive, *Not* on the Negative 49

THOUGHT #3 : Focus on What You Can Do,
Not on What You Cannot Do 93

THOUGHT #4 : Focus on What You Have,
Not on What You Do Not Have 117

THOUGHT #5 : Focus on the Present,
Not on the Past and Future 137

THOUGHT #6 : Focus on What You Need,
Not on What You Want 163

THOUGHT #7 : Focus on What You Can Give,
Not on What You Can Take 187

Elevate Your Life with the *7 Thoughts* 209

A Note on Mental Health 225

Let's Change a Life Together 229

Thank You 231

Did You Learn Something New? 232

An Invitation to the "Master Your Mind" Community
(on Facebook) 233

More Books by I. C. Robledo 234

An Introduction to the 7 Thoughts to Live Your Life By

"We are shaped by our thoughts; we become what we think. When the mind is pure, joy follows like a shadow that never leaves."
– Buddha

What are the Ultimate Goals of this Book?

The goal of *7 Thoughts to Live Your Life By* is to transcend the goals of self-improvement books. What does this mean? Whether your goal is happiness, peace, finding your purpose, spiritual healing, productivity, success, wisdom, sociability, clear thinking, or something else that involves improving yourself, I believe you will find what you need here. Ultimately, this book will provide you with a unifying framework to help you maximize your potential.

Let's consider what separates this book from the many others which you may have read.

You may have heard that in warfare, or in strategy games, that there are *tactics* and there are *strategies*. Tactics are generally seen as concrete actions you can take to solve a specific problem. Self-development books generally focus on this. A focus on tactics can be helpful because often, you have a specific problem, and you need it solved. For example, if you want help with making new friends, then you may find a book that deals with this specific issue.

In contrast, strategies are built around *not* solving one particular problem, but in planning and putting yourself in the best position to deal with *any* problems that may arise. Although this book does include tactics and concrete tips, it includes them in a way that is ultimately strategic, and that will help you put yourself in the best position to deal with the primary obstacles of your life. *7 Thoughts to Live Your Life By* may not show you how to solve your immediate problem, but it will be your toolkit for understanding how to make the best use of your mind, and to use it to its full powers to solve your everyday problems. This approach should ultimately be more effective.

A further goal of this book will be to help you attain clarity and focus of the mind. We live in a world overloaded with information – which can be found via the internet, books, news, television, radio, gurus, and so forth. With so much information available, and so much new information being made available daily, it can be difficult to create a calm and focused mind. Our minds tend to go in all directions and accomplish little in the end.

The fundamental idea of *7 Thoughts to Live Your Life By* is that if we could calm the mind and focus on what truly mattered, then we would be much happier, more at peace, and ultimately able to live a life full of meaning.

As a final point, I would like to mention that I have occasionally received emails from people who will explain to me what their life problem is. I have noticed that typically their misery comes from *not* having applied the *7 Thoughts* in their lives. In many cases this is simply because they are not aware of their existence. I have observed this quite often, in fact, and I have found it frustrating to know that their issues could be resolved in a straightforward manner if only they had the same insights that I have had – with this book, now of course it is possible for you to gain those insights.

Before delving into the Thoughts, allow me to share some of my background with you in the following section.

A Destructive Force Within…

Now, let's begin with my life, and what drove me to write this book in the first place.

I spent, or perhaps *wasted*, years of my life. I spent that time in a negative haze, with a dark cloud hanging over me. I had problems with being sociable, so I assumed that people didn't enjoy being with me and that they did not like me. It was a great struggle for me to be around people, because I felt that they were thinking negatively about me. I didn't sense it at the time, but my issue was more with my internal negativity, rather than any true negativity on their part. Sometimes, people even asked me, "Why are you so negative? What is wrong?" But I never had a good answer. My belief was that reality actually was negative and terrible, and that I simply had to deal with it. I didn't understand that I was being consumed by my own negativity at the time – and that my way of seeing life didn't represent reality.

However maladaptive my negative way of thinking was, by my early twenties I was getting used to it. I thought that the negativity was a part of who I was – that it was in my personality. My life had evolved into a bad habit of seeing, thinking, and doing in a negative way. Of course, I was not happy about this – but at the same time, I didn't see any other options. I didn't know any other way to be. I felt entrapped, but I couldn't grasp any way out of the reality that I had created for myself.

This way of being lasted for many years, and then came the toughest period of my life. I had applied to a graduate school program in industrial-organizational psychology. I had a deep doubt within me, realizing that I would be tested beyond what I could even imagine. A part of me knew that I was not ready for this program, but I applied anyway. On paper, I was an excellent student, but my communication skills were quite poor, and I was worried about this. Nonetheless, I was accepted into the program.

In the first week, I realized that this would be the biggest challenge of my life. However, the work itself wasn't overly difficult, intellectually. Rather, there was so much work that needed to be done, that there appeared to be no end in sight to it. For example, there was a heavy load of course work, multiple research projects, learning to use statistical programs, management of undergraduate researchers, many administrative tasks, and a variety of meetings per week on research topics, all while I was adjusting to living in a new state.

My biggest battle at the time, however, was not the work itself, nor in adjusting to the new location. It was in learning to deal with my own overwhelming negativity. The force of it was becoming greater and greater, as it gained in power under the increasing pressures and stresses of my life.

Even in the first few weeks of the program, I did not think that I could deal with all of the work. I felt like I was being suffocated under all of it. I had so much to do and learn that it was overwhelming, beyond anything I could have expected. I had begun to lose confidence that I would be able to do all the tasks required of me. Failure was often on my mind – I sensed that it was inevitable.

After several months in the program, I felt defeated. I was keeping up with the work demands, but my mind was telling me that I was going to fail, over and over, and I was not happy. Work occupied my mind all day long, and when it was time to sleep, I could not stop thinking about it. Generally, I would only sleep a few hours per night. I was also losing weight, and I was already thin when the program had begun. A big sign that my mind was malfunctioning was that I was forgetting very simple things. I would forget meeting times and sometimes I could not recall what someone had said to me only moments earlier.

At my worst, my mind was occupied with incessant negative thoughts about myself – which is clearly counterproductive. I may have been sitting in a meeting, and my mind would wander into negative thoughts. I couldn't focus on anything else but this negativity. Eventually, I did not want to be in the program any longer. But I continued with it nonetheless.

After a few more months it was winter break. I should have been happy, but instead I found myself bedridden. I spent most of the days in bed, not because of a physical ailment – but because of a mental one. The negativity inside of me was on permanent full throttle now. Imagine getting into your car, putting it in neutral, and then putting your foot down on the gas all the way. The engine is revving so hard that it sounds like it could break, but the car isn't going anywhere. This is what my mind and my life had become. My mind was working in overdrive to the point of self-destruction, but I was not making progress. The fact that I was in bed, unable to do much of anything, only reinforced the negative thoughts I had had – that I was truly not going to be able to continue with the program.

As a simple example of just how bad things were, I found it difficult to do a basic task such as brushing my teeth – even this took all of my energy to accomplish. Sometimes I would feel good that I had managed to do this on my own, and then I would go back to bed and wonder:

If this is what I have stooped to, how will I ever continue with this graduate program? How will I ever finish my degree? If brushing my teeth is difficult, how can I learn advanced statistics and manage undergraduate students, or even show up to meetings or classes?

I thought seriously about whether it was even worth it to continue. But I somehow realized that my mind wasn't working properly, and I didn't feel qualified to make such a big decision in that state of mind, so I didn't quit.

In reality, the program was becoming less of a concern – my life itself was now my biggest problem. If I continued to deteriorate at this rate, I would have much bigger problems than just finishing a graduate program.

After this lowest of lows, spending most of my days in bed, I decided to finally get some help and I went to my doctor. I was given some tests, and he explained that I had major depressive disorder *and* dysthymia. He prescribed some antidepressants and he told me to start seeing a clinical psychologist to receive some counseling. He said that in my deeply depressed state, it was critical that I take the medication *and* attend the counseling. Either one alone would not be sufficient.

After a few weeks of following the treatment, I was well enough to function again. I could do basic tasks, but it was still a struggle to operate at the higher level that the graduate program required. After a few months, I was doing fine. I was no longer overwhelmed by a self-created negativity, and I was able to do all of my work without much trouble.

The true healing would take many years, however. The medication and therapy helped to reset my mind and body, but I was not truly healed. I still needed to learn to control my mind to prevent this from ever happening again. After a couple of years on the treatment plan, with the aid of my doctor and therapist, I stopped taking the medication and I stopped going to counseling. I felt the need to do this so that I could control my own destiny fully. I wanted to be sure that *I* was the master of my own mind, and that I didn't need to rely on either medication or counseling. I intuitively knew that I didn't need it—my biggest problem was a self-created negativity, and therefore I could learn to control it.

In the months after stopping treatment I didn't feel worse, but I still didn't feel happy, or like I was on a path that I looked forward to pursuing. I wasn't overwhelmed with negativity, but I didn't view this alone as a true success. It's as much of a success as you would say being absent of pain is a success. The achievement of not being profoundly empty or sad just wasn't enough. There needed to be more to life than just this. *I wanted something more.*

As an important note, if you want to stop taking a medication or stop a counseling program, be sure to discuss this with your medical and counseling professionals first. There can be great risks with stopping either one suddenly, depending on your situation.

The Path to True Healing

Realizing that my life was not yet on its proper course, I reflected on why some things had gone so wrongly. In fact, I often reflected on this. Clearly, my focus on everything negative had not helped. It seemed as if my natural focus on the negative had spiraled out of control, and I was unable to tame it after it had gained a certain degree of momentum. However, I felt like there was something more that I was missing, so I continued to reflect, day after day. Ultimately, this was not bringing me any new insights, and so I realized that I needed to change my approach.

Then I began meditating. I believed that doing this could help me to control my own negativity, which it did. But ultimately, what surprised me was that I sometimes had deep insights into myself or about the world that arose through these meditations. My system was that I would enter a peaceful meditative state, and in a deep focused state I was often able to perceive lucidly. Then, I would ask myself a question on how to live a better life, and how to overcome my problems.

One day while meditating, these Thoughts all flooded into me:

1. **Focus on what you can control,** *not* **on what you cannot control**
2. **Focus on the positive,** *not* **the negative**
3. **Focus on what you can do,** *not* **on what you cannot do**
4. **Focus on what you have,** *not* **on what you do not have**
5. **Focus on the present,** *not* **on the past and future**
6. **Focus on what you need,** *not* **on what you want**
7. **Focus on what you can give,** *not* **on what you can take**

I believe my mind had synthesized *all* of the mistakes I had made in my life. It had examined the numerous mistakes and missteps that had led me into a life of growing negativity, to the point that this negative force had become greater than the force of my own true self. In meditation, my mind realized that it was itself, *my own mind*, which had become the enemy. Thus, through an intuitive and synthetic process, I came up with these Thoughts to help prevent the mind from becoming a destructive force, and to allow it to flourish and become a constructive force – a force for good rather than a force for bad.

Essentially, in my personal life, I had been focusing on the opposite of these Thoughts, and so intuitively, my mind must have realized that this had been the source of my problems. I needed to have a dynamic shift, a shift of the mind into the opposite of what it had once been. It would be a transformative process. My challenge would be to flip my focus completely – and to turn everything around. I wrote down the *Thoughts*, and I began using them as a guide post. I started living my life by the 7 Thoughts, and from then on, my life was never the same. True change didn't happen overnight. It took years, in fact, but every time I repeated these thoughts to myself, as if they were a mantra, I felt at peace sensing that I was moving along the right path. Things would be alright in the end.

Why are These Thoughts So Important?

I find that when I stray from these Thoughts, and I allow myself to go with the crowds and fall into negative patterns and worry about what is outside of my control and dwell on the past, that things start to fall apart. Depression and anxiety are not far off. Often, I diverge from the Thoughts just a little bit, then a little bit more, and then I find that I am quickly becoming lost at sea – surrounded by a turbulent storm. Luckily, when I have noticed this, I have been able to navigate myself back to safety. This has happened several times, and I am only more convinced that to live a good life, it is critical to follow these Thoughts *every day*. Following these Thoughts forces me to be fully conscious about my thoughts, so that I can learn to attract the good thoughts and to let the bad ones flow out of me. When I stop giving fuel and energy to those bad thoughts, they tend to go away in time.

I am aware that sometimes authors get excited about an idea or a system that they have only used briefly, and they want to write a book about it. I would like to be clear that the background of this book is nothing like that. I originally had these Thoughts 7 years before the publication of this book. In that time, I have reflected on these Thoughts deeply, and incorporated them into my life. At times, I would briefly forget about them, but every time I did I realized that I had made a big mistake, and I would incorporate them into my life once again.

Our true task, which this book shall help with, is to *turn the destructive mind into a constructive mind*. This isn't to say that your whole mind is destructive, but perhaps parts of it are. Then, wouldn't it be best to flip those parts of your mind around and make them work for you in a positive way?

Of course it would.

Before continuing, I need to mention that since coming up with the Thoughts in meditation, I have realized that they are everywhere. They appear in religious texts, philosophical works, fables and parables, psychological studies, and in everyday maxims or sayings that people say. The fact that they appear over and over in a wide range of important texts, and in the words of a wide range of gurus throughout a span of millennia, shows just how important these Thoughts are. As you can see, I did not discover these Thoughts. They were always there, and I simply rediscovered them for myself. They are common and yet hidden away, because most of us don't follow them since we are bombarded by thousands of thoughts and pieces of information daily. It is time for us to clear the clutter, and to prioritize the Thoughts in our lives.

The Top Three Ingredients to Living the Good Life

A key aim of the *7 Thoughts to Live Your Life By* is to help you to live a good life. Here, I will discuss the top three ingredients that you will need for this: Purpose, Success, and Happiness.

Purpose

What is your purpose? Do you know? What is your WHY? Why do you do anything? Only you can figure this out, but if you have not, I would urge you to view this as the central issue of your life until you do figure it out. Understand that your purpose is not limited to a field of study. For instance, your purpose is not to be a doctor, it is to save lives. Your purpose is not to be an architect, it is to build the most beautiful or the safest building that ever existed. Your purpose is not to be an artist, it is to make the world come to life with beautiful art that makes people wonder about what is possible. The book *Mastery* by Robert Greene helped me not only to realize my purpose, but to have the courage to pursue it whole-heartedly.

Create your own *life purpose statement*. Think about what you truly want to get out of life, and how you can get to that point. What do you want to provide for others? What is the most personally fulfilling thing you could do? If you feel like you need more experience or knowledge to figure out your purpose, acquire it. For example, you may contact an expert and interview him or ask how you can be of help. An expert is more likely to help you learn if you commit to helping him, rather than if you focus on what he will give to you. Through helping, of course, you will learn greatly.

Make your life purpose statement short and direct. I would recommend that it be either one sentence or two short sentences if possible. When you have crafted it, put it in a prominent place where you cannot forget about it. Also, it does not have to be static. In time, you may choose to modify it or even start over from scratch.

Success

"Your level of success will seldom exceed your level of personal development." – Jim Rohn

Ultimately, we all need to define what success means for us. However, I believe most people have a limited view of what success is, and I would urge you to consider my definition below.

Success = Energy + Morals + Purpose

A foundation of your success will be your energy levels. We tend to take this for granted, but you need to be feeling good and have a strong vitality to be in the best position to succeed. Even for those of us who appear to be in great general health, we should always dedicate some time to keeping ourselves healthy and energetic. As we know, this involves a combination of eating healthy, exercise, sleeping well, and stress management. In general, I would also recommend that you do things that make you feel more energized and avoid those that do not. For instance, if driving aggravates you and drains your energy, it may be better to find someone who can drive you, or to ride a bike.

Next, success is about sticking to moral principles, because if you don't, then any "success" you achieve is tainted by misdeeds you may have committed to meet that achievement. At its core, morality is about treating others as you would like to be treated, and about being truthful with yourself and others. There is not a specific moral code that you must follow, rather, it will be important for you to do what you know to be right on your path to success.

Also, success ultimately happens when you are living out your life's purpose. You may be in a life situation that makes it difficult to live out your purpose – but I believe it will be worth pursuing with all of your heart and might. If you don't, you will always wonder what could have been. You must understand that true success comes when you find a way to live your purpose, even if that purpose is not defined by your job. The two do not always overlap. A key way to live out your purpose is to make the most of any special skills you may have, or your gift (See 7th Thought). But ultimately, only you can decide your true purpose.

Happiness

To me, happiness is being free to express yourself, it is being as healthy as you can be, alert, energetic, and able to feel at a full range of emotion and not restricted to always being rational or emotional. Happiness is to be in sync with your morals, to be in the pursuit of meeting your purpose, and to be your true self, not a false created self that you feel other people want you to be. Of course, happiness is to have love in your life, which could come from family or a spouse, or with other people that you develop close connections with. To be happy, it is not required that you have a favorable life. It is possible for a dying person to be happy, or even someone who is in prison to be happy. Happiness is doing your best, but ultimately accepting yourself, people, and situations as they are. It means being able to control your mind (See 1st Thought) so that you can be in a positive state (See 2nd Thought), regardless of the situation or environment.

The ancient Greeks believed that happiness was something that could not be fully judged about a person until their death. Someone may be happy in one moment or another, but to know if they were truly happy, we must look at their full life.

Your Thoughts Will Rule Your Life – Choose them Carefully

"Happiness is when what you think, what you say, and what you do are in harmony." – Mahatma Gandhi

I present the quote above as a reminder. Many of us have thoughts that are completely incongruent with the person that we truly want to be. But rather than change those original thoughts, we learn to justify our actions. Instead, we should go back to square one and examine the thoughts that we choose to have, because from there, they have great influence over what we say and do.

Many of us think of thoughts as *just thoughts*. They are harmless, perhaps even meaningless, you may think. I will show you that this is far from being true.

In reality, the sum of your thoughts leads to the sum of your actions, which leads to the sum of who you are. Many people understand that they are the sum of their choices and of their actions. What they don't always fully understand is that they are also the sum of their thoughts. Their thoughts lead to their actions.

Allow me to elaborate.

Your thoughts will become manifest in your expressions (e.g., such as facial expressions) – and your expressions are contagious. If you have a sad expression, it is much more likely you will make others feel this too. If you smile happily, you may have this effect on those around you as well.

Your thoughts will become what you say – and what you say is mimicked by others. Just as your expressions are contagious, so is what you say. Have you ever noticed that you may hear a new phrase, and soon after this you start to hear it all of the time? A catchy expression is mimicked by many and it quickly becomes the go-to catch phrase of the public.

Your thoughts will become your actions – which model behaviors for others. Actions are also contagious. If you spend a great deal of time with someone, you may find that you start to do some of the same things. Even if this person has strange or unique habits, you may find yourself mimicking this person, perhaps unconsciously.

Your actions will become reactions in others – and those reactions will mimic the original action. For instance, aggression tends to create the reaction of aggression. Love tends to create the reaction of love. Fear in one person tends to spread that fear to those who are nearby. It does not always work this way, but if you perform an action, you are much more likely to create that same reaction in someone else.

In summary, your thoughts will become contagious in others – in the form of expressions, words, actions, and reactions that will pass on as if an echo. When you speak in a small room, you will hear your own echo. Similarly, everything you think, say, and do forms a sort of echo reaction in the world around you. You will not be able to perceive that echo, because unlike an echo of sound that reflects back at you almost immediately, the echo of your thoughts and actions passes through the world slowly, but it ripples through the universe for eternity. In fact, much of what we are doing today is the result of the echoes of prior generations – what they thought, what they said, and what they did.

Have you ever noticed that there is truth to the saying that we become our parents? Of course, we get to choose our own actions and we are not limited to being who our parents are, but in times of stress or when we are tired or don't have time to think, our default actions are likely to fall back to what we have seen our parents do. You may find yourself repeating phrases that your parents would say, in the same situations that they would have said them. This is an example of the echoes through time, of people's thoughts, words, and actions. Perhaps your children will feel the same, and use the same phrases at those same moments, and perhaps their children too. Our thoughts, words and actions transcend ourselves, spreading as if a virus – this can be a good thing if they are positive and bad if they are negative.

Understand that what you think ends up creating the entire world around you. Of course, this effect is hard to see because of the slow echoing, but also because we are all playing a role in the thoughts, words, and actions that get passed on, and which ultimately become contagious. Since we are one person of many billions in this world, we feel like what we think, say, and do does not matter. But it does. Your thoughts can propel you forward or drag you down, and they can do the same for countless other people – having a big impact on the people who you surround yourself with.

The implications here can run deep. The world becomes influenced by what you think, and it reacts to you based on what you think of the world. What you think is reflected back onto you. If you are in love with the world, you receive a loving energy back. If you are angry at the world, you receive an angry energy back. Thus, you must mind your thoughts. Be careful what you think, because what you focus on and what you think will take up a bigger space in your life.

Remember this: Mind your mind. Mind your thinking. What we think has a way of manifesting itself into reality.

The 7 Thoughts that Help Us to Live the Good Life

The following are the 7 Thoughts which will be the focus of this book:

1. Focus on what you can control, *not* on what you cannot control
2. Focus on the positive, *not* the negative
3. Focus on what you can do, *not* on what you cannot do
4. Focus on what you have, *not* on what you do not have
5. Focus on the present, *not* on the past and future
6. Focus on what you need, *not* on what you want
7. Focus on what you can give, *not* on what you can take

While I came upon these thoughts during a meditative session, I have thought about them deeply and I would like to explain the logic of these Thoughts, and why they are ordered in this way.

By focusing on **what you can control**, you immediately prevent yourself from wasting your time, life, and energy on matters that are out of your influence and control. With this focus, you will realize that the #1 thing that you can control is your mind, and your mind performs much better when you **focus on the positive** instead of on the negative. However, if there is a problem in front of you, perhaps one that you have negative feelings about, then you must **focus on what you can do** to resolve this problem. Your focus will be on what is within your power. Just remember that what you can do is limited by what you have, or your resources. Thus, you must **focus on what you have**, because this is all that you can work with to resolve your problems. Logically, if you focus on what you have, then you need to **focus on the present moment** in your life, because this is all that you truly have. The past is done, and the future is uncertain. The present is where you influence the world around you and where you have control. In the present moment, you must keep perspective and prioritize what truly matters in your life – thus, **focus on what you need** above what you want. What you do not need, you may give away, to **give back to the world** which has given much to you.

Inspirational Figures

I always find it helpful to keep some inspirational figures in mind, to remember that we are capable of much more than we think we are. Here are just a few brief stories of people who have triumphed even when the odds were against them. I hope they inspire you as much as they have inspired me.

Malala Yousafzai

Malala is a young woman who stood up for the rights of girls like herself to pursue education, even when she was still a child living in Pakistan, a place where this was not a freely given right. What did she get for saying that all girls should have the right to education? Sadly, she was attacked, *receiving a bullet to the head.* Suddenly, Malala was fighting for her life. This attack proved the great dangers that any girl in Pakistan may face just for speaking her mind. Luckily, she did survive and recover from this horrible attack. Despite the incident, Malala never wavered in her message. Ultimately, she went on to win the Nobel Peace Prize in 2014, where she was commended for her "struggle against the suppression of children and young people and for the right of all children to education." Malala along with her Malala Fund – a nonprofit organization, has helped rebuild schools and is active in helping girls to have the right and the path to pursue 12 years of "free, safe, quality education."

William Kamkwamba

William was a young boy who grew up in extreme poverty in Malawi, Africa. His family was very poor and at one point he was unable to afford $80 that was required for him to attend school. Incredibly, this boy living in immense poverty was able to build a windmill to bring electric power to his village with a bare minimum of resources. Some materials that he used to do this were blue gum trees, bicycle parts, and other materials he had gathered from a local scrapyard. Importantly, he had often visited the village library and discovered books with pictures of windmills in them, which ultimately helped him to build his own. In 2014, he graduated from Dartmouth College and according to his *About* page on www.williamkamkwamba.com, "He is now working with Wider Net to develop an appropriate technology curriculum that will allow people to bridge the gap between 'knowing' and 'doing'."

Cruz Robledo

Cruz was a young man with a 7th grade education growing up in Mexico – making him the most educated person from his village at the time, in the early 1960s. His dream was to go to the US to pursue greater opportunities. In the small village where he was raised, education beyond around the 3rd grade level was considered a luxury that generally could not be afforded. However, Cruz showed a promising aptitude in school, and his father supported him financially so that he could reach the 7th grade. Unfortunately, the pressures on his father with raising a large family made it infeasible for him to continue funding Cruz's education beyond this point.

At 17 years old, Cruz decided to go to the US to pursue greater opportunities. He learned English and went to night school, and then he applied to Purdue University. They offered him admission, and he was immensely grateful for this opportunity. Being a student there was the greatest challenge of his life, as he realized that his educational background left him far behind the other students. By this point he was working full time, taking a full load of courses, and he had a family to support as well. Ultimately, despite the high level of challenge, he did graduate with his B.S. in agriculture. After working in his industry for a decade in the US, he started his own business in Mexico, where he provided and continues to provide research services for leading universities, companies, and institutions around the world. This man is my father, as you may have noticed that we have the same last name.

In all of these stories, we have individuals who were far, far behind everyone else. They had *fewer opportunities*, not more, and yet they managed to lead successful and fulfilling lives. Ultimately, they surpassed the majority of people who would have had many more advantages. I find it important to always keep these types of stories in mind. Whenever you doubt yourself and your situation, understand that many people have thrived even when having come from practically nothing.

Now that you know what is possible when you put your mind to it, I believe that you are in the right frame of mind to begin learning about the 7 Thoughts to Live Your Life By.

Before You Continue . . .

As a thank you for reading, I want you to have a free guide called:

Step Up Your Learning: Free Tools to Learn Almost Anything

Although learning tools may appear to be a completely different topic than the one this book covers, I believe strongly that we should *always* be learning something so that we can meet our full potential as human beings. Remember that you are always able to learn about any topic that is important to you. I recommend that you focus on areas you are curious about, or that can help you to get one step closer to your dream job or dream life.

This guide stems from my own experiences of using a variety of learning sites and resources. In it, you will discover the best places to go for learning at no cost. Also, I'll explain which resources are best for you, depending on your learning goals.

You can download this free guide as a PDF by typing this website into your browser: http://mentalmax.net/EN

Now, let's get back on topic.

THOUGHT #1

Focus on What You Can Control, *Not* on What You Cannot Control

"You have power over your mind – not outside events. Realize this, and you will find strength." – Marcus Aurelius

The Most Important Thought in This Book

When people approach me for advice with their problems, at least half of the time, the problem lacks focus. A problem can only really be a problem if there is something you can control to meet an objective, and if you have a clear goal. However, examples of the problem types I tend to hear about are: "I can't believe my wife still wants us to go to Las Vegas even though I told her that I hate it there." "My kid wants to study art, and he doesn't understand that there just isn't much money in it – he should go into engineering." "I'm sick of feeling alone. Why don't people ever give me a chance?" The common issue in these problems is that there is a desire to control someone or something that is in fact out of our control. Because we are social creatures, we badly want to have control over others' beliefs, thoughts, and actions, but it doesn't work. This desire leads to misery.

At its core, this Thought is critically important because it is about making sure *not* to waste your time, life, and energy on pursuits that will lead you nowhere. In order to properly live your life, you first have to conserve it against the things that you are *not* able to influence. Even if something is very important, if you cannot influence it, then you should find a way to put it outside of your mind. You will be much better off focusing on the things you *are* capable of having some control over.

I believe this is the most important Thought in the book because it is quite easy to waste much of our time and energy on pursuits that lead nowhere. If we had just thought at the beginning about whether we could control something in the first place, it could have saved us the heartache. The principle seems simple, but if applied well, it will prove highly effective in helping you to live a better life.

What is in Your Power to Control?

Control means that you are able to create an outcome of your choosing in a highly reliable way. Many of us feel that we have control, but often what we mean is that we have influence. We can guide people or events in the direction that we please, but "control" would be too strong of a word to use in such cases.

Consider what you actually have control over in your life. Here is a list:

Your mind – You have control over your thoughts, your beliefs, your desires, and your expectations.

Your words – You have control over what you say and don't say, and how you say it.

Your actions – You have control over what you do with your time, what job you perform, and how you spend your money. Also, even when you are in a negative emotional state such as being angry or sad, it is ultimately up to you to decide which actions you will take.

Your emotions – Emotions are not easy to control, but this does not mean that they cannot be controlled. It just means that it takes practice. William James, the father of American psychology, has expressed that by controlling our actions we can control our emotions. For example, to feel happy, act as if you were happy. In this case, you may smile, laugh, and talk in a more animated way. However, trying to control an emotion directly through telling yourself to feel a certain way, is unlikely to work.

Your relationships – You have control over what types of relationships you enter, what types of relationships you choose to invest your time and energy in, how you treat others, and how you allow other people to treat you. But of course, you cannot control another person.

What is _Not_ Within Your Power to Control?

The things we *can't* control

The reality is that there is much more that is *outside* of our control than there is *within* our control. Here we will see all that is *not* within our power to control:

The consequences of your actions — No matter how much you think you have something figured out, and how perfect you think your predictive abilities are, there is always something outside of your control that can create a different result than what you expected. We must expect the unexpected, because even under seemingly perfect conditions, we cannot control outcomes.

Other people's minds — We are not able to control other people's thoughts, beliefs, or their desires.

Other people's words — We are not able to control what other people say, don't say, or how they say things.

Other people's actions and reactions — What someone else chooses to do, or how they react to something that you choose to do, is ultimately outside of your control.

Other people's emotions — Many people have a difficult time controlling their own emotions, so clearly you will be unable to have control over someone else's emotions. You may do things that influence people's emotions, but ultimately, you cannot control them.

Nature — We are not able to control wild animals, the weather, earthquakes, tornadoes, or other natural phenomena.

The universe at large — We are not able to control the way the planets or the stars move, or the rules (e.g., mathematical formulas) that the universe operates under.

The past and the future — The past has already happened and cannot be changed, and the future is uncertain, and not something that you will be able to predict, let alone control. Of course, we can take actions that influence the future, which is well-advised, but we do not have control over what will happen in the future.

You control little, yet you do it with great power

Understand that you are only in control of yourself in this massive universe. The more that you realize this, the smaller you may feel, knowing that your level of control is quite minute. However, you should be aware that you still have great power in what you are able to control. As a person, wherever you go, you will always have some level of control over what happens to you. And this is the most important type of control that you could want to have – as it gives you great power over yourself and your immediate surroundings.

Sometimes you have partial control, or what we refer to as influence

As you can see, the level of control that you have is not black and white. Obviously, you may have influence over other people's minds, words, and actions, but you cannot truly control how other people think, what they say, and how they act. Even for the most agreeable person that you meet, who appears to agree with everything that you say – you do not control him. There is always a chance that this person doesn't agree with you at all, but that he enjoys the attention that you give when he appears to agree. Or perhaps the person does not like any kind of conflict, and so he agrees with everyone publicly on matters that he may disagree with privately. It is true that you may have some influence over others, but in the end, you cannot control them.

Let go of those things you cannot control – liberate yourself

I would like you to now release yourself from the responsibility of the things you cannot control.

Just take a deep breath and let it all go, right now. Go ahead. Don't overthink it. Just do it.

Of course, I cannot force you to let it go. You must do it for yourself. The more you have clung to a pattern of feeling the need to control that which cannot be controlled, the harder it will be for you to learn to let these things go. It may not happen immediately for you – it may take time, and that is okay.

The human mind can be perplexing because we trick ourselves in two contradictory ways. We think we have more control than we do – and that we can control things that are in fact uncontrollable, such as other people. And we don't seem to realize that through the power of our own minds and thoughts, we can create the life and reality that we would like to have. There is no need to control all of those things that are outside of our power to control. Knowing how to control ourselves is *more* than enough. We can control our thoughts, our desires, what we say, the actions that we take, and how we respond to setbacks. This is all we need.

We must learn *not* to agonize over what we cannot control, and instead to focus on controlling fully that which *is* in our power to control.

When you free yourself from this unnecessary weight, it may feel like a literal weight off of your shoulders. You will be liberated. You will then be able to say what you think, and influence events to the extent that you are able, but you will accept the final outcomes as they happen, because you will be aware that those outcomes are outside of your control, and therefore they are not worth worrying about.

For anything outside of your control in your life, even though you may not want it there, you must learn to move along with it fluidly, as if you were swimming with a current and not against it. Fighting what is outside your control is like swimming against the strong current of the sea. You will work quite hard, working up a sweat, crying, screaming, yet getting nowhere. Instead, if we can learn to swim, dance, or roll with the things we cannot control, we will be much better off.

Remember this: Resisting the things we cannot control does not change them or make them any easier to deal with.

"Humans won the lotto. We control the planet." – Gary Vaynerchuk

Gary Vaynerchuk is the founder of VaynerMedia, author, and podcaster who freely gives advice to aspiring entrepreneurs. He likes to remind us whenever we are complaining and feeling like there is no way to make progress in life, that as a species we are at the top when it comes to having dominance and freedom on this planet. If you put the quality of life of all species on a hierarchy, we would be number 1. This is because we are creating or rearranging the environment as we like to have it. We planted the forests, selectively bred animals guiding them to become what we wanted them to be, and we created civilizations and organizations to meet our wants and needs. And despite the problems that humanity has created, we are the only species that is in the position to fix those problems.

Gary's point with saying "Humans won the lotto. We control the planet," is that there are such a massive number of creatures and lifeforms on this planet, that to be human is a truly special occurrence. He estimates that the odds of being human are 400 trillion to one. You could have been a dog, a rock, a plant, a blade of grass, or a bacterium, for example. Keep in mind that unless your parents are both from the same small town, they could have quite easily never met, which would have made your existence impossible. The point here is for us to remember that life is all a great gift. Estimating the true odds of our existence as human beings is perhaps impossible, but the 400 trillion to one figure is a good reminder that the odds must be incredibly low that we were ever going to be here in the first place. Therefore, we must be grateful.

As human beings, we are in control of our lives. In fact, as mentioned above, we are also dictating how the Earth itself operates – as much as is possible for us to do so. Yet, many of us still sit back and complain about all that is going wrong. Some people will say, "With mega-rich people such as Donald Trump who were born into wealth, how can I compete?" Or they will say, "With being born in a neighborhood filled with violence and poverty, what do I have to look forward to?" Or they will say, "I'm just not enjoying life. I get up, go to work, go home, watch TV, and go to sleep. What else is there?" In all cases what there is, is the fact that you are human and have a great amount of control over yourself, and therefore over your immediate situation. Of course, there are obstacles and it is not easy. But what option does a dog have? What option does a blade of grass have? What option does a bacterium have? You have options, which is a special thing, although we tend to forget it. Don't forget it.

Are you Giving Them Too Much Control?

Computers, smartphones, tablets, etc.

Often, I will go out, and I will notice that a family of husband, wife, and a few kids are out to dinner, but they are all glued to their devices. Sometimes they even have a special colorful tablet to give to their young children. Seeing this sometimes makes me question, are we controlling these devices, or have they begun to take control over us? Are they making us feel like we need to have them at all times?

The issue isn't that we are using these devices. After all, they are tools that serve a purpose – often for entertainment or for work. But when we feel that we must always use these devices, and we lose the ability to live our lives without them, this means that we are no longer living life on our own terms. We are being controlled by something outside of ourselves.

We are used to thinking about addictions to drugs, but people can become addicted to anything. It is only in recent history that we have had constant access to our small computer devices – tablets and smartphones, and perhaps we have not yet had the time to see how much they are influencing or controlling us. It is also only in recent times that we have had access to virtually all known information in our pockets, at any time of day. This is also something we become addicted to, and that tends to influence us.

Keep in mind that the apps that we use are typically designed to be addictive. Often, they will use gamification – having game-like features to make you want to engage with them more and more. And any apps you use will present you with important news and notifications, making you feel the need to open them again and again. It is up to us to be aware, and to be more cautious about what types of apps, software, devices, and products we allow into our lives. We must control them, not the other way around.

Parents and family members or friends

Is there someone in your life who you look up to, who means well and always seems to help you when you have a problem? If so, this can be good, but there may be a point where you are giving up too much control. Be aware that you could end up being guided in the direction that this person wants you to go in, rather than feeling free to go in the direction that would truly be best for you. We must be careful in these situations, because people often mean well, but if we allow it, they may become too controlling over our lives.

Of course, the younger you are, the more helpful it may be to follow the guidance of your parents or older siblings. But as an adult, at a certain point you need to make your own choices and live with them. This is the only way you can be sure that you are fully in control. Ultimately, it is you who lives with your choices and their consequences, not anyone else. It is perfectly fine to listen to feedback or suggestions, but always understand that the final choice of what you do with your life is yours only. The path of doing what someone else says, then blaming them if something goes wrong is not a fruitful one. You must own your actions and live with the results that they produce. Remember that helpful feedback and suggestions are good. It is when people order you with authority, or when they attempt to manipulate your thoughts and feelings, that you will have a problem and need to break free of their hold on you.

The news

Is the news shaping the way that you think more than it should? Marilyn vos Savant, recognized as former Guinness world record holder for the highest IQ, (a category which has been retired) has made an interesting point in her tweets, stating that news apps tend to show us more of the types of news stories that we prefer to see. This makes sense, until you think of the consequences of such a thing. Because news apps do this, you are likely to see more and more stories with a similar perspective or bias, which are then likely to reinforce your viewpoints more and more. Unfortunately, this can make you feel *less open* to new possibilities and ways of seeing the world. In effect, your news app will be controlling you into perceiving the world through a narrow lens, because of your original preferences.

Savant has also stated that the news is becoming more about commentary and persuasion rather than just straightforward reporting of the daily events. I fully agree with this. Often when I have seen the news, it has involved pundits arguing their viewpoints. This is fine, but if the purpose of the news were to inform the viewer of worldly events, then it would be more reasonable to make an attempt at unbiased reporting of the facts. Instead, often a news agency will actually have an agenda that they are trying to convince the viewer of. For instance, most news outlets lean toward a political party – and everything that they report on may have this bias.

Do not be fooled into thinking that you are receiving objective, truthful information from the news. You must remember that the information is biased, and so allowing it to shape your whole view of the world would be a great mistake. At the very least, seek your news from different outlets to make sure to compare different viewpoints and then make up your own mind as to what the reality is. Or perhaps tune into the news less – and spend that time living your life instead.

Your heroes and role models

I used to have role models. I think everyone has had them at some point in their lives. But there are some inherent problems with having role models. For example, they tend to be able to manipulate you easily because you look up to them, which of course could put you in a vulnerable position. I would advise you not to allow a model to have direct control over you, and do not assume that everything they do is right. It is a mistake to follow your models without thinking critically about what it is that you are doing. You must think more deeply about how you live your life. Don't perform your actions automatically, without thought, for this will create many problems for you.

When it comes to models, no one meets a perfect standard of morality and excellence in every way, and in fact the two can be inversely related. The more excellence one attains, the more power usually, and the more power, the more chances to abuse that power. This doesn't make powerful people immoral necessarily, but having power does tend to corrupt the people who are not disciplined enough to wield it properly.

Understand that having role models is a setup for disappointment. Often, you will start to see the person who is your model as bigger than life, as the epitome of all that is good, and this rarely reflects the reality. We all have our faults, and a much more useful strategy is to have *role actions*. Find the actions that you believe in which could benefit your life in some way and adopt those for yourself. Be willing to explore the *role thoughts* that are beneficial as well. This will mean having deeper conversations with people you may admire to figure out not just what they do, but how they think through problems. In exploring their thoughts, you will learn to adopt their way of thinking when it suits you. Also, you may learn general principles that you can use to help solve many different types of problems.

Commercials and advertisements

Turn on the radio, ads. Go online, ads. Go out on the streets, ads. Look at the bumper stickers of a vehicle, ads. I have even seen ads tattooed onto someone's neck. Ads are everywhere, and even with so many competing ads, they still appear to be a profitable investment for the companies that use them. If it wasn't worth it, they wouldn't put up the ads in the first place.

With every day that passes, there are more and more of them. We don't find the presence of ads to be too strange or uncomfortable in the present day, but perhaps if they get to the point of invading our personal space, or guiding our every thought, we will notice.

I know that you may think that all of these ads don't influence you. But they are likely having a greater effect on us than we would like to think. If nothing else, they are filling our minds with junk in the background all of the time. Even if you are not interested in any of the ads, then your mind is always busy filtering them out. With your mind constantly preoccupied, this could wear you out and then lead you to make poor decisions later. Every time you see an ad, you have to make a decision – to buy or not to buy. You probably make thousands of decisions every day just because of ads, without realizing it. This wears you down, perhaps causing you to give in to impulses and buy things that you didn't need.

We tend to think that ads have no control over us, but what if they do? What if we have seen some ads from certain companies so often that we develop personal connections to them? They make us comfortable. Perhaps we do not enjoy the product that the ad mentions any more than other similar products, but with a lifetime of associations built around a particular product, our minds build deeper and deeper connections with it. The mind may eventually form more connections with a product than we have to some family members – such as an aunt, uncle, or cousin. Do we enjoy the product because we enjoy the product, or do we enjoy it because we have been manipulated into enjoying it, by having a great wealth of mental or neural connections created for us through the simulated experiences we have had via the advertisements?

Manipulators and toxic people

Some people like to control those around them. These people enjoy having others do what they want them to do. These controlling people tend to understand people's desires and fears, and they will use that knowledge to their advantage, in order to manipulate the people around them. You will need to learn to spot when someone is attempting to take control of you, and to release yourself from their grasp. These people have such a strong need for control that if you put up some resistance, they may quickly look for someone else who will play along with their games.

It is important to have your own aims, your own purpose and objectives that you are pursuing, so that you will not be so easily controlled by someone who wishes to use you.

Be aware that when a manipulator cannot get his way, he may resort to controlling your emotions, for that is easier to do. He may create situations to make you worried or scared. Or he may say offensive things in order to make you angry or to get you to react. The manipulator lives to elicit reactions, and relishes in making you behave in a way that makes you look bad or inferior. Again, for this reason it is important to spot the manipulator early on, to understand that his desire for control is dangerous, and that this will be a person you should distance yourself from.

Destructive behaviors

On the *Dr. Phil* show, the psychologist Dr. Phil often had clients who had developed destructive habits and behaviors. His response was typically: "What are you getting out of this behavior?" His point was that people tend to engage in destructive activities in order to gain something. As humans, everything we do is meant to have some kind of benefit. Otherwise we wouldn't have done it. For example, people drink alcohol excessively in order to escape the reality of their problems. They get into fights because they like to be feared and respected rather than ignored. They drive much faster than the speed limit to impress their friends. Realize the positive outcomes that you are getting from your negative behaviors, and then find a better, truly positive way to get that outcome.

What can we do when these destructive behaviors start to take hold of us? This is the key. We need to stop them early, before they have the chance to ruin our lives. As soon as possible, we must remove the bad influences with surgical precision and replace them with positive influences. For instance, I used to eat sugary snacks quite often. I was hooked. Sometimes I would skip a meal and just eat the sugar-loaded snacks. Then, I realized the harmful effects of sugar, and so I stopped eating all unnecessary sugars for two years. This was despite the fact that I had become addicted to them. Through my realization that they were harmful, I recalibrated myself, learning to enjoy natural sugars from fruits, which are good for you. I also sought out more interesting and varied meals, rather than just relying on sweets. After two years, I allowed myself to eat sugar, but it was much easier to eat it only occasionally by this point. I had reset my mind and body to where I didn't feel the need to eat too much of it.

You may be wondering about how you could quit something that is bad for you so quickly. Everyone is different, but what worked for me was thinking rationally. I knew that I did not want to become diabetic or suffer any other health issues – so I decided to mostly remove unnecessary sugars from my diet. When I saw sugar, instead of thinking about the great taste, I reminded myself that this leads to outcomes that I don't want. I wanted to be free from illness more than I wanted to taste something sweet, so the choice to stop eating sugar was rather simple. But perhaps even more importantly, I banned myself from buying sugary snacks – I banned myself from even going through the "candy and sweets" aisle in the supermarket. How can you ban yourself from something? It's simple. Just remember that you are truly in control. Anytime you decide to do something that is harmful to yourself and you know that it is harmful, you decided to do this and no one else. Similarly, only you can decide *not* to do something, and then stick to it.

Remember this: Be careful with who or what you are giving up control to. Once you have given up control to forces outside of yourself, it can become difficult to reclaim it for yourself.

Protect Yourself When You Know You Lack Control

Be careful with thinking "I'll just do this one more time, and that's it" – it becomes an endless cycle

I enjoy playing games, but I find that the worst thing I can do is build up momentum, playing game after game. For example, if I have played 10 games of speed chess online when I should have been working, the momentum of that allows me to say, "I've already wasted half an hour, so what does it matter if I continue to play and waste another half hour?" To prevent this line of thought, we have to learn to say to ourselves *in advance*, "I will only allow myself to do this X times, or for Y minutes. Then I must stop." If you break this agreement with yourself, there must be a consequence. Make yourself tell your coworkers or your spouse about it. Or ban yourself from the activity for a week, due to your inability to control yourself. We ground children, and this helps to guide their behavior, so perhaps we need to occasionally ground ourselves as well. You may be surprised to find this temporary ban to be quite welcome. It will help to reset your brain and take away the intense desire and addiction, so that you can regain a sense of your true priorities.

If you find yourself wasting too much time, I would urge you to put rules in writing for what you will and will not allow from yourself. When you write something down, it becomes more real, and you are much more likely to follow through on it. What helps me when I find that I am wasting too much time and that I have gotten off track, is I will write down *everything* that I do in the course of a day. I will write down every task that I engage in, and from what periods of time. This helps make it so that you cannot lie to yourself – you are forced to see where your time is going, and then you can begin to correct any misuses of it. If this exercise seems like a waste of time, I will assure you that it is not. In fact, this activity will show you how much time you are truly wasting.

(not unlike a food journal)

Exercise caution with how you are being rewarded – "Rewards" that drive you away from your life purpose are ultimately punishments

I have played a game on my phone, where the game itself rewards me for playing more. If I open the game every several hours, I will be able to accept rewards that the game is ready to give me. But if I only open the game once per day, I will receive much less in rewards. I am sure that this motivates the game's players to come back and check on it quite often, spending more and more time with it.

At first when I began playing this game, it would constantly be on my mind. *I should check if it's time for my reward*, I would think, and I would check back every couple of hours or so. But of course, in time I decided that I needed to take control. I should play the game just for fun, and not allow its design to control my behavior. I continued to enjoy the game, but I would only check on it when I had free time, on my own terms. I stopped thinking about the rewards of the game because I understood that I should not waste my time by concerning myself with when I can receive rewards from an app.

Understand that the most addictive apps and games are designed in this way not by coincidence, but because they use our own psychology against us. In the 1950s, psychologist B. F. Skinner researched the nature of *variable-ratio rewards*. This type of reward means that sometimes you receive a reward for a given action, but other times you do not. And the more times you perform the action, the more rewards you will receive overall. For example, sometimes you get a reward for pulling the lever of a slot machine, and sometimes you do not. There is no predictable pattern for when you will receive the reward. In this case, the reward is to win more money than you put into the machine, of course. Some of the most addictive games implement such features – gambling, lotteries, and some video games as well. This psychological effect is so powerful that some people will lose control, and their lives will become ruled by needing to seek out these variable-rewards. Their lives will be controlled by their addiction.

Someone who is not in full control must learn to avoid such games altogether. The key to know if you are addicted to something isn't just in your actions of course – ask yourself if something is constantly on your mind. If it is, I recommend a break from it for at least several days if not a week. This will help you to regain control and realize that you don't need it. Then if you wish, you can come back to it later, on your own terms.

Be cautious with how you allow rewards to guide your behavior. Do not allow yourself to be rewarded too often for negative behaviors. If you do, these behaviors will become a larger and larger part of your life, and you will become someone who you did not wish to be.

Control is *Not* All or Nothing – You May Have Partial Control

Think probabilistically

For most things in life, we only have partial control. This means that there are forces outside of us which will ultimately decide the outcome. For this reason, it is important that we get into the habit of thinking in probabilities to get a more accurate view of life. To practice this, if you are given a tough assignment at work, try predicting your chances of success. If you want to ask someone on a date, predict the chance that the response will be "Yes". For greater challenges, when you meet someone, predict what her occupation is before she has the chance to tell you, and state the probability that you would be correct. Many people I have met think in a more binary fashion – they predict that something will or will not happen, but they are not precise enough to calculate the probability that the outcome will occur. For this reason, most people are surprised when they find out that they have made a wrong prediction. However, when you think probabilistically, you tend to get surprised less often. Even if I am fairly confident in something, I may predict that it has an 80% chance of happening. This is only 4 out of 5 times. If my prediction turned out to be wrong, I may be a bit disappointed, but I would not be shocked by this. This is a skill we should all practice from time to time. You will find that the more you practice probabilistic thinking, the more accurate your predictions become.

Examples of probabilistic thinking

The following are three brief case examples on how to implement probabilistic thinking. Practicing this for yourself will help you to learn how much control you have over situations.

Case 1

Billy is a 12-year-old child without many friends, and I want to help him make more of them. My plan is to take him to the movies on weekends and become his friend to help him build confidence in himself. With more confidence, he will be more likely to make new friends. I calculate that there is a 40% probability that Billy will make new friends because of this. My expectation is somewhat low because there may be reasons outside of his confidence for his lack of friends. Perhaps he has poor hygiene, bad manners, or he has irritating habits, for example.

Case 2

My aunt has a broken leg, so I am going to visit her weekly and clean her house so that she can heal faster and worry less. I calculate that there is a 60%probability that this will work. I expect this to help my aunt, but if she is not willing to have a positive attitude, or if she assumes it is my duty to help and that it is not a favor, then my assistance may not help her as much.

Case 3

Miranda is struggling with her geometry class which just began two weeks ago. She is a smart, motivated, and hard worker, and this is the only class she is doing poorly in. I am going to tutor her so that she can earn at least a B in the course. I calculate that there is an 80% probability of this working. In this case, I have a high confidence in Miranda's abilities, but if she gets sick or if she gets distracted with friends or loses focus in some way, then she may not improve as much as I predicted.

An important point is that you should practice justifying why you chose a particular probability. Even if it is just a quick justification, as in the ones presented in the examples above, this will help you to be as accurate as you can be in your predictions. After the event has transpired, you should check how accurate your predictions ended up being. Did you tend to expect the chances of success to be much higher than they actually ended up being? If so, then you know that you need to lower those numbers in your future predictions. With every prediction you make, your ability to estimate the probabilities properly will improve.

This means you will become better at estimating how much control you have over a given situation.

We do not have 100% control, not even over our own minds

I know that many of us feel like we are in complete control over our minds, but the truth is that we are not. One quick way to show this is that most people experience some degree of negative self-talk. We judge and talk to ourselves or think about ourselves in a hurtful way. Why would we do this to ourselves on purpose? For the people who do it too much it can even become a form of self-abuse. The explanation is that we are not in full control over our minds. If we were, we would choose not to think about ourselves in negative ways.

The other way to show that we are not in full control is that no matter what task you are doing, you will not be able to maintain 100% focus on what you are doing for very long. The mind tends to wander – which means you lose control of it. Some people can focus intensely for an hour or more. For others, 5 minutes of focus may be a great challenge. Either way, we all have our limits and start to lose control over our own minds after a certain point.

We should also be mindful of our emotions. Sometimes when we become emotional, we may lose control of ourselves for a short while. We may even end up doing things that we regret because of this. Other ways that we lose control of the mind are through mindless habits, or from tiring out the mind through performing intense work, or through people who "push our buttons" and provoke us to react emotionally.

Impact and importance

When you are going to take action, ask yourself, "Is this something that can have a great impact and is this of great importance?" Higher impact means that it could have a big influence for a large number of people. Higher importance means that this is something essential or critical in some way.

In the CNBC article, *Elon Musk: Starting SpaceX and Tesla were the 'dumbest things to do'*, Elon Musk has said, "I gave basically both SpaceX and Tesla from the beginning a probability of less than 10 percent likelihood to succeed." However, he went forward and accepted these chances because he believed that these projects were important and that they could have a high impact upon the world. For example, with Tesla, electric cars can help us reduce our dependence on oil, which will be more important for the future since oil is nonrenewable. And with SpaceX, we may be able to travel to Mars and beyond, which could be more important in the event of a life-threatening catastrophe here on Earth, or even as a larger plan to have humans colonize space.

My advice is to get involved with plans that add up to higher numbers when you add up the impact, importance, and probability of success. And if you are in a situation where you can tolerate a lower probability of success, then I would suggest *not* dismissing such ideas too quickly. Those ideas may have great potential to become breakthroughs.

Ultimately, we need to become comfortable with the fact that we have limited control. However, we should understand that within our narrow range of what we can control, we have a great deal of power. We may not have much influence and control over the world as a whole, but we are able to develop a great deal of control and influence over our personal worlds.

The Extremes: Control Everything, Control Nothing, or Take the Middle Way

We want control because we don't want to feel powerless. We want to feel that we can always improve our situation. The problem is when we develop an obsessive need to control everything around us. Rather, we must learn to let go of the things that we cannot control. Also, we have to learn that not everything we can control is truly worth controlling.

Some people become obsessive with wanting to control everything, and this brings troubles. They can never be satisfied because they are never able to attain full control over their environment. On the other hand, some people wish to let go of as much control as they can, and this brings troubles too. They can never be satisfied, because in giving up all control to others, they are unlikely to get the things that they truly want and need.

In this case, the middle path is the right path. The key point of focusing on what you can control is that focusing on the noncontrollable things is a complete waste of your time and energy. However, if you find yourself getting upset because you are not fully in control over *everything* in your life, or upset because you have control over *nothing* in your life, then it will be time for you to take a step back and reevaluate the situation. You will then see that the middle path of figuring out what is truly worth controlling, and then pursuing control over those things, will be the best path forward. As to the rest, we must let it go.

Exercises

Meditate

Sit in a quiet place and be aware of your thoughts without needing to judge them as good or bad. Let them pass through you instead of hanging onto them. Do this to learn to see your thoughts in a more neutral way, and to *not* allow your wild thoughts to control you. In meditation, you will learn to see that your mind has a natural tendency to wander into the past and future, worry and stress, daydreaming and hysterical fantasies (e.g., when you imagine a traumatic scenario happening). Ultimately, meditation will help you to see that you are not in full control of your mind, but through training, you will be able to gain power over your own mind.

Do breathing exercises

Practice abdominal breathing, which is to breathe through your lower lungs. When you do this, your stomach area will expand on inhalation, rather than your upper chest. Breathe in and out deeply and slowly, focusing on each breath. Make sure that your stomach area is expanding and contracting, and not your upper chest. Breathing exercises will help you to reduce anxiety, to relax, and to control your emotions. When we are anxious and uncomfortable, we tend to breathe more shallowly, through our upper chest, and so we must learn to have some level of conscious control over our own breathing. If you practice this regularly, you will be in a calmer state, and better able to handle the problems that you must face.

Do muscle relaxation exercises

Start with one end of your body, such as with your toes, and tense them up for 10 seconds, then relax them for 30 seconds. Do the same thing, but progress through the rest of your body – through your calves, legs, stomach, chest, arms, hands, shoulders, and so on. In the course of a day we will bear a variety of stresses. Through weeks and months, our bodies will build up tension in reaction to this stress. Of course, this tension can affect your psyche, making you moody, anxious, or irritable. To help maintain control over your body and mind and to be in a more relaxed state, it helps to periodically do muscle relaxation exercises. An alternative is to get a professional massage.

Make a list of things you can and cannot control

Take a sheet of paper and divide it into three parts. In the first part, write down all the things that are within your control. On the second part, write down all of the things that are *not* within your control. On the third part, write down all of the things that are within your ability to influence, but are not within your full control. Be sure to consider things that you have tried to control in the past, but that were actually out of your control. Also, write down the things that are within your control but where you had neglected to control them in the past. This will help to always remind you what is truly worth attempting to control, and what things are not worth it at all. For the list to help you further, you may rank your items in order of importance for each section.

Make probabilistic predictions of what you expect to happen today

For everything you will attempt today, ask yourself what your probability of success is. Do this to improve your understanding of what level of influence, or partial control, you have in your day to day life. Predicting the probability that an outcome will occur can help you to learn to judge your influence over the world around you. Make predictions such as: *There is a 50% probability that I can jog for a mile without stopping.* Or, *there is a 70% probability that if I apologize for something I did, that I can repair a relationship.* It helps to write down your predictions, and then to write down the outcomes, so that you can judge your predictive abilities accurately. Recall that the more you do this, the better you will become at making more accurate predictions.

Practice the nonresponse

When someone does something that is meant to provoke a response from you, practice full control over your own mind. Rather than allowing yourself to become angered or offended by what someone has said or done, practice just being. This will put you in a state of not needing to be reactive. You are not a simple machine with buttons that can be pushed in a literal sense, where because someone says something mean, you must get mad. If someone makes a rude gesture to you, this does not mean that you must react with the same gesture or with offensive words back at the person. The way to show yourself and those around you that you truly are in control is to be able to *not react*. This may be a challenge at first, but in time you will master the nonreaction. You will be able to have no physical reaction, and no mental or emotional reaction to something that is meant to provoke you. Understand that if you always react automatically, then people will more easily provoke and manipulate you. Learn to master the nonreaction to escape their control and regain it for yourself. Do not mistake this as a passive process – it takes active control on your part to become master of yourself. Once you have mastered the nonreaction, you can smoothly continue with what you were doing before the interruption, and your day will be unaffected as a result. If you were in a good mood and telling jokes before the provocation, then you can continue in this way.

THOUGHT #2

Focus on the Positive, *Not* on the Negative

"It is during our darkest moments that we must focus to see the light."
— Aristotle

The Most Important Thing to Control

We just covered the importance of focusing on what you can control in your life. A reasonable next question to ask is, "What is the most important thing for you to control?" The answer is your mind. With controlling your mind, you can have great influence over your perceptions, your attitude, and you will be able to maintain a positive outlook even in difficult times. Understand that when you are able to use your mind to stay positive regardless of the circumstance, you will build resilience and toughness inside of you. You will then be in a position to conquer your dreams and fulfill your purpose.

What do we Mean by "Positive"?

Pleasure

Sometimes when we think about the positive, we think about pleasure. Of course, pleasure can be a positive experience, but when we seek pure pleasures at the expense of everything else, this is often negative. Typically, a person on this path will be impulsive and destructive. Someone who is driven in the pursuit of pure pleasures is likely to become obsessive and addicted, leading to their own destruction and causing great problems for anyone caught in their path.

One type of pleasure is hard drugs, which come with a higher risk of addiction, overdose, and death. Truly, any addiction can turn into a destructive pursuit of pure pleasure – whether it would be for drugs, hording, food, or something else, which can turn your life into a single-minded and meaningless pursuit, with a lack of concern for the people in your life. Another example of pure pleasure would be quite simple. It would be the extreme selfishness of only doing things you like, and only doing things that benefit yourself, often at the expense of others – to the point of being deceitful just to get what you want. This form of pleasure-seeking can have some benefits for yourself but leads to negative outcomes for others.

Long-term gratification

What I generally mean by positive experiences then is not pure pleasure. Although clearly some pleasures can be a part of a good and healthy life, the constant pursuit of pure pleasures tends to spiral us out of control. Long-term fulfilment, rather, is what is more worthwhile when we are pursuing the positive. These are behaviors that are much more likely to be gratifying not just in the present, but which we would look back on happily in the future as well.

Examples of what would be both positive and gratifying for the long-term is raising a child with good values, pursuing a purpose which is for the greater good and not just to meet a selfish desire, and to help someone in need without expecting anything in return. These types of experiences bring joy and meaning to our lives. Rather, the pure pleasures tend to give us a brief sense of meaningless elation. Understand that fulfilling positive experiences will end up giving us far more joy in the long run than a short-term pleasurable experience would.

What Positivity is *Not*

Getting what you want with *no* effort

In video games, we have something called cheat codes. These are special codes or sometimes hacks that are used, where you can receive rewards without needing to work for them. In real life, the equivalent would be if you could wake up tomorrow with 10 million dollars and with the most attractive person you ever met as your partner, and do no work whatsoever for this.

I will admit that when I was a child, I sometimes used cheat codes in video games. But every time I did, I was surprised to find that it was completely unfulfilling. Using the codes would ruin the game, and it would no longer be fun or enjoyable. When there is no challenge and rewards are given without merit, then there really is no purpose.

We must realize that if we hacked life somehow and got everything we desired, then instead of joy, we would likely feel joyless. In real life, unfortunately we see millions of people who are in an endless pursuit of pure pleasure, sometimes even until it kills them. But the cost of life is not an issue for them. If they are not in a pure state of pleasure, life no longer has meaning for them. They become blinded and controlled by their immediate desires.

When we get caught in the vicious addictive cycle, it can become too powerful to escape. People who feel empty and unfulfilled are much more likely to seek these pure pleasures and ultimately to become destructive. Instead, that emptiness should be filled with positivity, meaning, and purpose. Of course, this is not the easy path, but it is by far a better choice than going down a road that will ultimately lead to great pain and suffering for yourself and your loved ones.

Denying the reality of a negative circumstance

Being positive does not mean that you need to deny the reality of what is happening. It does not mean disregarding plainly obvious facts. Sometimes, terrible things happen and we have to comprehend that the situation is bad. However, there is always something we can do to influence a positive outcome. In a difficult circumstance, our task will be to search until we find those actions that we can take to help ourselves and to help others.

We must train the mind to see that no matter how hopeless a situation appears, there must always be a way forward, and we just have to find it. Even when facing such a circumstance, do not give up so easily. Giving up on your purpose, your dreams, or something that you need to do is the worst mistake you could make. Of course, mistakes often present learning opportunities – but giving up on yourself would be truly disastrous, shutting down opportunities for you to learn and grow.

What is Positivity Good for?

Before continuing, I would like to present you with some of the evidence for why positivity is so helpful in our lives.

Health

According to the Mayo Clinic article, *Positive Thinking: Stop negative self-talk to reduce stress,* "Researchers continue to explore the effects of positive thinking and optimism on health. Health benefits that positive thinking may provide include: increased life span, lower rates of depression, lower rates of distress, greater resistance to the common cold, better psychological and physical well-being, better cardiovascular health and reduced risk of death from cardiovascular disease, and better coping skills during hardships and times of stress."

As you can see, being in a positive state of mind generally has beneficial effects on your health.

Success

The best way to see how positivity influences success is with Carol Dweck's mindset theory. She is a professor of psychology at Stanford University. This is mindset theory in her own words from www.Mindsetonline.com:

"In a fixed mindset, people believe their basic qualities, like their intelligence or talent, are simply fixed traits. They spend their time documenting their intelligence or talent instead of developing them. They also believe that talent alone creates success – without effort. They're wrong.

In a growth mindset, people believe that their most basic abilities can be developed through dedication and hard work – brains and talent are just the starting point. This view creates a love of learning and a resilience that is essential for great accomplishment. Virtually all great people have had these qualities."

The key difference between these mindsets is that with the growth mindset, you are focusing on the positive, on your simple ability to improve in what you do. Understand that believing in your abilities and in your potential tends to result in positive outcomes. This is fairly logical when you consider the opposite. Someone who does *not* believe in his ability to accomplish much is unlikely to fully pursue his goals, and therefore is unlikely to be successful. A positive mindset of course will not cause you to succeed by itself, but it will help to provide you with the best chance.

Mood & attitude

Being positive and focusing on the positive will help to influence your mood, making you generally feel happier or at least content, rather than sad, empty, or miserable. And who would not want to be in a better mood? Being in a better mood means that you will tend to spread more joy to those around you, helping to create an atmosphere of people who are also in a good mood. This is certainly much better than the alternative, to be miserable and always looking at the negative side of things, creating a negative atmosphere everywhere you go.

Sociability

Strong friendships and family bonds are easier to build and maintain when you naturally look for positive things to say. If you don't believe this, then sit at a table with some friends and point out something negative about everyone. Or try talking constantly about negative stories you have read. You will likely find that you start getting invited out less and less. Looking for positive things to focus on and discuss, rather, helps to keep everyone in a good mood. When people are socializing, they generally want to get away from all the negativity and problems of life, not dwell on them. Rather than tell jokes at people's expense, tell jokes that make everyone laugh. Tease in a fun way rather than making sarcastic, biting comments.

Mental toughness and resilience

When you are in a positive state, or able to think more positively about situations, your mind will become tougher. Even if you suffer a setback or several setbacks in a day, you will learn to see these as events that you can overcome. You will come to understand that the setbacks you endure do not need to define you as a failure, and that they do not need to put you in a dark state. The more you practice positivity, the more resilient you will become. Just as lifting weights trains your body, practicing positivity will help you to build mental strength.

Peak performance

Positive thinking is critical at the highest levels of competition. When both you and your opponent are optimally trained, it can feel overwhelming to attempt to win a battle against such a fierce opponent. What can give you the edge in such a case? Simply the positive belief that you can find the right solutions to whatever situation may arise in your battle. In a 2013 interview with Charlie Rose, here is what Magnus Carlsen, world chess champion said: "I think there are plenty of players in history who have been immensely talented but they're just too pessimistic. They see too many dangers that are not there and so they cannot perform at the highest level." In chess, they call these *ghosts*. You see threats to your army on the board that are not legitimate, and so you prepare for those ghost threats, and then fail to have prepared for the true dangers. Of course, there is a balance of preparing for difficult times and situations, but of also ultimately believing that you are fully prepared to handle whatever comes your way. In competitive games and sports, positive thinking is a true asset.

Remember this: Positivity has immense benefits for your health, your ability to succeed, and your ability to perform at your peak. Negativity on the other hand, can influence us in the opposite direction.

What are You Taking in and Consuming?

Junk food for the mind

Just as there are good foods and bad, there is good mental consumption versus bad. Most of us understand that we should have a healthy diet, and so we aim to eat more fruits and vegetables, and to not eat too many preservatives or too much fast food. But many of us do not stop and think about all that we are consuming that is bad for the mind, for our emotional and spiritual health and wellbeing. For example, we may surround ourselves with chronic complainers, listen to news stories that make us feel the world is coming to an end, or we may have an employer who verbally abuses us on a daily basis. The reality is that this could be just as bad as eating nothing but a junk food diet. I will urge you *not* to feed your mind junk food. Understand that receiving too many negative inputs into your mind will tend to place you in a negative state of mind. When you receive more positive inputs than negative ones, you will tend to be in a positive state of mind.

Joyful versus toxic people

How many toxic or bitter people do you interact with daily? Do you know some people who no matter what is going on in their lives, they always have something negative to say about it? When they are miserable, everyone has to hear about what is going wrong. Whether they're overworked, stressed, having relationship troubles, or health problems, you hear about it day after day. Even if they are not talking to you about it directly, perhaps you hear this person in the background talking to other people about it. If you are a family member or coworker of such a person, you may feel as if you can't get away.

For many of us, having to listen to this type of thing becomes normal – it's a way of life that we deal with daily. The problem is that this takes a toll on you. Of course, I am not saying that you should never stand to listen to a single negative word. That is not the issue. People have legitimate problems and sometimes they have to discuss how to overcome them, or they may need to vent. Other times, noticing a problem can seem negative, but it can turn into a positive experience when people work toward resolving it.

The issue, however, is when there is negativity that serves no real need or purpose. This is something you should avoid surrounding yourself with. Complaining with the purpose of gaining attention or sympathy is just selfish when it is overdone, day after day. We may all do it occasionally, but to do this chronically is unproductive. For example, complaining can help the complainer to feel better, but ultimately it can drag everyone else down, putting them in a bad mood. Notice that chronic complainers often do not want or even pursue actual solutions to the problems they present. Instead, their stories present themselves as victims. They prefer to keep complaining and they become stuck in the victim role, rather than using their energy on making true progress. This is easier for them, because otherwise they would need to take action to try to improve the situation, and since they see themselves as victims, this does not seem worth it. Their thinking may be – "Why bother trying if it won't work out anyway."

This is a backward cycle that you do not want to get involved with. If you lash out at the chronic complainer, you give him another reason to complain and you reinforce his worldview that the world is a cruel place meant to give him a hard time. If you listen to him complain, you condone his behavior and provide him with sympathy simply through the act of listening, which means you reward him for complaining, making him likely to complain even more. The best option is to shut the person down politely. "Sorry, I'm busy at the moment." Of course, it isn't always so easy to escape. Finding a way to *not* give this person any attention or emotional satisfaction for their complaints will be vital, to avoid encouraging this behavior.

Relationships

Generally, relationships should be based on love, acceptance, and understanding, which is good and healthy. However, they can sometimes be based on distrust, dissatisfaction, and a lack of understanding, which of course is not good and healthy. We have to learn to attract the good kinds of relationships and to avoid the bad ones.

Think about who is in your life the most, from day to day. This will probably include people who you live with, whether they are your parents, a spouse, children, or possibly roommates. Some of your close relationships may also be with your coworkers or with superiors at work. These relationships tend to be very important because we spend a lot of time with these people, meaning that they can have a greater influence over us.

Be cautious if you find yourself surrounded by people who are insensitive to your needs. They may belittle you, be sarcastic, attack you verbally or even physically, actively get in the way of your pursuits, start intense arguments with you, and so forth. Depending on the frequency and intensity of these, they can create a toxic environment for you.

Something to be aware of is that healthy relationships have issues too. Don't worry that if you have an intense argument with someone, that this automatically means the relationship is toxic. This isn't necessarily the case. The problem is when you feel drained and agonize over interactions with certain people. Keep in mind that in some families or in some relationships, arguments may be a normal part of life, and it can be an effect of personalities that clash, but who still care for each other. In fact, some people may have a way of bonding through their arguments. The issue is if someone becomes distraught and deeply troubled through chronic arguments. If such a thing occurs often, we may have a toxic relationship which is in need of repair.

If you have found yourself holding all of your thoughts inside and becoming resentful in order to keep the peace, you should realize that this isn't the best path either. In some cases, it is reasonable to disagree with someone and possibly even to argue. I will ask that you consider the middle path. Do not always argue, and do not always hold in your feelings and keep them to yourself. Perhaps the best option is to state how you feel without needing to argue about it. Be who you are and hold your own viewpoints and allow others to be who they are. Some people get intensely argumentative because ultimately, they wish to control others, and people of course cannot be controlled so easily.

Note that if you find yourself in an overly toxic environment that is harming you, you should consider leaving that environment if possible. This may involve stopping an activity, changing your workplace, or even changing homes. The more drastic the choice would be, the more deeply you should consider if it is truly worth it to leave the environment, or if there is another way to repair the situation. For instance, if you have an issue with a sibling, discussing the matter with another family member could help. Or if you have an issue with a fellow worker, discussing this with your employer could help.

Even if you are not contributing to the toxicity in any way, you will suffer through everyday exposure to it. For this reason, you may consider leaving such environments even when it is not your fault.

Remember this: Allow others to be who they are, and be who you are. You do not need to agree with everyone, and everyone does not need to agree with you.

The news

The vast majority of news stories cover what is bad and wrong with the world. For those people who watch the news the most, they may develop a grim outlook on life. Some examples of the common types of topics covered are: war, acts of violence, natural disasters, deaths of important people, controversies and scandals, health scares (e.g., contaminated food, aggressive viruses, increasing rates of illnesses), etc.

Spending too much time watching the news doesn't make a lot of sense. The time you use watching the news and learning about all the negativity in the world could have been spent on taking action rather than just passively listening to problems. Also, the themes of the news repeat over and over – every time you watch the news, you already know what is going to happen – it will most likely be one of the common scenarios mentioned in the above paragraph.

These are some of my reflections after watching the news:

We focus so much on the horrors of life, when we need to put more focus on the heroes that survive those horrors. We need to focus less on the gunman, and more on the gunshot survivor. Less on the message of the oppressor, and more on the message of peace and prosperity. What we focus on becomes our reality.

Music

Perhaps an argument can be made that listening to music which focuses on a bad mood, on depression, hate, anger, anxiety, etc., could be useful to vent these emotions. However, we need to be careful to not allow such mood-perpetuating music to keep us locked into an unfavorable and unnecessary state of mind. Sometimes, certain music can even romanticize or make it seem acceptable to be in a certain negative state. If overdone, this can be harmful and make us feel stuck. Be aware that we can get addicted to emotions such as sadness, anger, hate, or even love and happiness. Instead of getting hooked on negative emotions, I would generally advise listening to more positive and upbeat music. Listen to what makes you feel good, not to what drags you down.

The environment

Be careful of the environment that you are in, because we often become a product of our environment. If you are always around loud and discordant music, you may become perpetually anxious. If you are in a place that is messy and disordered, with graffiti and litter all over, your mind may become disordered and you may feel that you lack purpose. If you are often surrounded by chronic complainers, you may become more like them, day by day. Be careful of what you surround yourself with because it can be difficult to overcome such forces. Keep in mind the environments you spend the most time with – such as your home life and close relationships, and your workplace. Ask yourself: *Are they environments where I feel positive energy or are they just draining me?*

The *Betterfly* and the *Bitterfly* Effects

What are you spreading?

Are you spreading "better" or are you spreading "bitter"? Good or bad? Joy or sadness?

The traditional idea of the *Butterfly Effect* says that if a butterfly flaps its wings on one part of the world, the effects of that may be felt on the other side of the world in the form of a hurricane. A small input (e.g., butterfly flapping its wings) can result in a dramatically larger output later on (e.g., a hurricane).

By *Betterfly Effect*, I mean to say that when you think or do something positive, the effects may be felt on the other side of the world.

By *Bitterfly Effect*, I mean to say that when you think or do something negative, the effects may be felt on the other side of the world.

These effects are far more important than many of us will realize. Whether we are in positive states or negative states, most of us are not fully aware or conscious of what our mental states are producing in the world. As an example, has anyone ever done something so nice for you, or said something so nice about you, that it completely transformed your day? Did your whole day feel as if it were filled with love and joy, and nothing could go wrong? I bet you have. But here is the interesting part. Did you find yourself, unconsciously perhaps, also being kinder to others, and wanting to do the right thing more than you normally would have? You may have smiled more than usual. Maybe someone said that you were glowing.

This positive energy that others bless us with is so powerful that it rubs off on others. It spreads. One person can spread it to multiple people, and those multiple people can spread it to more multiples of people, and so on, having a magnified effect. Positive energy is likely more powerful in its ability to spread than any virus. Yet, similarly as with the virus, we don't see the energy itself spreading. Also, we don't always realize who has "infected" us with the positive or negative energy.

Have you ever noticed that after someone dies, sometimes people will say "I will keep him forever alive in my thoughts"? This may be truer than we know. When someone dies, every single thing this person thought and did continues to ripple and echo through the world, influencing people in ways that go undetected. In some ways, we never die. Our thoughts and their powers never fully die. Personally, I relate to some of the great people – from Buddha to Jesus to Leonardo da Vinci to Mahatma Gandhi, as well as Albert Einstein, Mother Theresa, and Martin Luther King, Jr. For all of the great people that I learn about, I feel like they are alive somehow in my mind. They are kept alive inside of me, and in countless others, because their powerful ideas continue to live on.

Ask yourself: Are you spreading *better* or are you spreading *bitter*. And remember that what you choose to spread can make all the difference in the world.

The Daily Drama

A fascination with the negative, the dark, and the drama

Have you noticed that most people seem drawn to the darkness? When there is a horrible car accident, we can't help but look over to see what happened, even though we know it cannot be good. People enjoy gossip, talking about the bad things happening in other people's lives. We watch violent TV shows or movies, attracted somehow to the extreme and dark depths of human nature.

I call this general fascination with the negative and the darkness, and how we are attracted to it, *The Daily Drama*. This is my name for it because I have noticed that many of us create a lot of drama in our own lives – we experience this daily, yet we don't even seem to realize that *we* are a primary reason for its existence.

We can end the drama, often by tuning out of whatever is causing it. Is it a personal desire to always have attention on yourself? Is it a colleague or a friend? Is it your overreaction to any minor event that you did not expect? We can learn healthier ways to acquire attention or learn to overcome our need for this attention. We can minimize communications with the colleague or friend, and we can learn that our overreactions make things worse. We may fear disconnecting from the drama, thinking that we will make things worse by ignoring it or by *not* giving it our full attention. But often, one drama arises, then it is corrected or forgotten. Then another drama arises, and the cycle repeats, again and again. We do not need to worry – the drama will always be alive and well. It is ourselves that we must take care of.

If this daily drama rules your life where every day is filled with it, I would urge you to break the cycle. Understand that you are playing a role in the drama by how you react to it, and that it is not fully out of your control.

Ask yourself: Am I going to feed the drama? Or am I going to allow it to die a quiet death, without feeding it any further?

A matter of survival

Why are we attracted to the negativity and the darkness?

By having some darkness in us, we are better able to identify it in others and to protect ourselves from it. For example, *The Prince* by Niccolo Machiavelli and *The 48 Laws of Power* by Robert Greene were both written on the theme of gaining power and using manipulative tactics to get what you want. However, they were not necessarily written with the view that you must do dark things, but also with the understanding that you must at least be aware that there are people out there willing to use dark means to get what they want from you. And thus, if you understand their intentions, you can prevent the use of these manipulative tactics on yourself.

We have to understand the darkness to overcome the darkness. If you do not understand it, you risk succumbing to it. The issue is that our minds sometimes dwell on the darkness, and become stuck in it, plagued by it. This is when we know that we have a problem.

Stop Comparing Yourself to Others

Seeing all that is bad in ourselves

One of the greatest lessons I have learned that helped to extinguish many of my miseries, was to stop comparing myself to everyone else. When we compare, we tend to focus on consequences, on results of actions, and we fail to remember that results are out of our full control. Recall that you can control your actions, but you will lack full control over the consequences of those actions. For example, you may notice that someone is highly skilled socially, that she has a brand-new car, or that she has a wonderful spouse, while your life may seem inadequate by comparison. The explanation for all of this may be quite simple. Perhaps this person is ten years older than you and she had much more time to work on her social skills, to save money to buy her car, and to learn hard lessons through many prior failed relationships. But we do not compare all of this because we do not see it. We only compare ourselves with what we see now, which are consequences of actions and events. This is a mistake.

Keep in mind that in our comparisons, we tend to see everything that is bad about ourselves. Most of us don't brag about how great we are compared to everyone else. Instead, we focus on the bad. When we are not doing as well as someone else, we feel as if we are failing. Comparing is dangerous because you end up focusing on things that distract you and put you in a bad mood, and this sets you up for falling further behind in your goals. On this path, you will risk succumbing to a vicious cycle where you continue to feel inferior. Understand that you have not had the same life as this other person, and so it is not fair to compare. Perhaps she had certain advantages that you did not have. Perhaps she had a different set of talents than you do. In such cases, it is unfair to expect the same level of accomplishments from yourself.

Compare yourself to yourself

If you are unable to get out of the habit of making comparisons, and you feel that you must compare yourself to something, then a useful tip is to compare yourself to yourself. This can work because the point isn't to beat yourself up over flaws in your abilities. Instead, as you grow and improve, you can look back and notice that you have improved compared to where you used to be. It is more important to be continuously improving, than it is to be perfect at anything you do. For that reason, comparisons to yourself can be quite valuable. Generally, you should not do this too often. Perhaps doing this every 6 months or a year could be useful. More often than every 3 months would likely be too much to be helpful. In your comparisons to yourself, you may ask if you are in a better position than you were. If so, be happy about it. If not, ask yourself if you did everything in your power to make progress. Understand that when you are doing your best, there is nothing to be upset about.

The Runaway Train of Negativity

The mind can quite easily go out of control with negative, depressive, anxious, and paranoid thoughts if we are not fully conscious of what it is doing. The following are some examples of the negative thoughts that the mind can produce when it is in the process of going out of control.

They're out to get me

Everyone else wants me to fail because they don't like me. Or maybe they're jealous of me, but either way they want me to fail. I know they're planning to sabotage and ruin me.

No one likes me

People don't like me and they never want to give me a chance. This is because I'm not as attractive as them, I don't have as much money, I'm not the right gender, they don't like people of my ethnicity, they hate my personality....

They think I'm dumb

I don't know as much as them about some topics and sometimes I get distracted and make mistakes, so everyone thinks I'm dumb.

No one wants to help me

It's not fair that no one wants to help me. I always help them with everything. No matter what I do for them, nobody wants to help me when I need it.

They don't appreciate me

Everyone takes me for granted and they expect me to do what they want, but when I do help them, they are not the least bit grateful for what I did.

I would like you to notice the harmful effects of using words such as "everyone," "no one," "they," "never," and "always," Words that overgeneralize are rarely describing reality as it is, instead they are exaggerating it, and giving the appearance of things being worse (or better) than they actually are.

Learn to observe and identify the above types of thoughts in yourself. Understand that they do not reflect reality – and when you have them, challenge yourself to produce a more accurate thought.

For example, instead of the maladaptive thoughts listed above, you may think: *Some of my colleagues are unable to help me even though I have helped them plenty of times in the past. Perhaps they do not have the time right now, and I can ask them again later.*

Or, *I sense that some people are looking down on me and they expect me to fail. Realistically, I know that I have the skills I need – that is why I was hired to work at this company. I must not allow them to bother me. Also, I may have misread them – perhaps they are not expecting me to fail.*

Overcoming the Runaway Train of Negativity

The phantom fear

Understand that the mind creates the objects of our fears everywhere that we go. When we watch too many crime shows, everyone in our real life becomes a possible suspect. When we are scared of snakes, every strange sound or shape is a snake ready to pop out. When we fear that we are not good enough for the person we are in a relationship with, every time he or she says, "We have to talk," we believe that a breakup is imminent. We must learn to control and overcome our fears, or they can wreak havoc on our lives.

The stories we tell ourselves

We breathe life into the stories that we craft about ourselves. If a young man believes that he is set up for failure because his father abandoned him as a child, then that will forever weigh him down. We have to ask: Are we going to empower narratives that do us harm, or those that lift us up higher? What if a person whose father abandoned him instead thinks: *I'm stronger for having gone through this experience. My mother took the role of a father-figure in my life, and I took on the role of a father too in helping to raise some of my younger siblings. In having overcome this situation, I am a better person.* The stories we tell ourselves, and whether they empower us and fill us with positivity, or disempower us and fill us with negativity, will make all the difference.

Regain control of the mind that has lost its way

When your mind is out of control with seeing the bad in everything, to the point that your own mind is working against you, you have to do something about it. Perhaps you notice that you're always in a bad mood. Perhaps you find it hard to function because there are so many depressing, anxiety-producing, and stressful ideas running through your head all at once.

Consider some of these approaches for helping to reset your mind: Talk it out with someone you trust, exercise, be with nature, spend time with children or pets, spend time with loved ones, meditate, or shower in cold water. An alternative is to examine your problems realistically and consider the worst-case scenarios to prove to yourself that you will be fine no matter what happens. In looking at problems realistically, for example, a failed marriage can seem quite troubling, but the worst-case scenario is a divorce and your ability to start fresh, not being weighed down by all the problems of your marriage. As another example, a failure to meet an extremely difficult deadline at work may get you fired, but it would release you from the unrealistic demands of your employer. When you actually consider the worst-case scenario, you often see that it isn't as bad as you thought. In many cases, the worst possible scenario will bring relief.

Of course, if you have a longstanding issue that is getting in the way of living a full and productive life, your best option will be to seek professional help – seeing a doctor, psychologist, or therapist, for example.

"The beast was loose!"

Many, many years ago on a cold dark winter, I was in a depressed state, and I realized that I needed to do something to help myself. I decided to take a walk around the neighborhood in hopes of resetting my mind.

I was walking through the neighborhood consumed by all of my life problems – I was falling behind in work, I lived a solitary life and struggled to make friends, and I generally was not happy with the direction of my life at that point. As I walked, I suddenly noticed something in front of me, barking loudly and forcefully. It was an angry, massive dog. It was on the sidewalk, clearly *not* held back by a collar or any kind of restraint – *the beast was loose!* The whole universe shrunk to just me and this big angry dog. It barked at me menacingly – and I could sense it asking: *What are you going to do? I'm ready for a fight, are you?*

My mind jolted out of its depression because it was forced to. I needed to think, and depression is slow and foggy. It's not good for thinking. I looked around and there were no other people outside. It was just the two of us. I was only half a mile away from my home, but the distance might as well have been to the moon. I didn't doubt that this dog could tear deeply into my flesh if its heart desired, and importantly, it could do this before I would have the opportunity to take more than a few steps.

In a flash, I synthesized everything I had ever heard about survival and animals, mostly from the nature programs I had viewed. I decided that my best option was to turn away slowly and to walk away at a normal pace, to show the dog that I was not a threat. Also, this would demonstrate that I was *not* running away scared – as I believe that many animals instinctively chase the scared prey. My guess was that the dog was being territorial, protecting its space. I had come onto its territory and it was not happy. The dog continued to bark at me menacingly as I walked away. As I listened to its barks fading, I could tell that it was not following me. I never looked back, and I made it home fine.

When I arrived at home, I felt relieved from my depressive symptoms because I had been brought fully into the moment. I had ceased to think about all of my miserable problems over and over.

I cannot recommend that you find an angry dog to cure your problems, but there is likely some value in finding something that is challenging and engages your mind and body fully, and that may even get your adrenaline flowing.

The irrational mind

I would not claim that we are incapable of being rational – obviously, we can be. What I would say is that the natural baseline level of the mind is not rational. In times of stress, we will struggle to be rational. As children, we are not rational. Thus, I would urge you not to assume that all of your thoughts are sensible and rational. This would be a mistake.

How can we guard ourselves from our own tendencies for irrational thinking? Consider a system that is becoming more common with guarding the public from politicians who make dishonest statements.

The system is simply fact checking. Rather than taking the politicians at their word for everything they say, we now have fact checkers who can tell us whether the statements made were accurate or not.

I would urge you to give your thoughts about as much respect as you would a statement from a politician who has not been fact checked. Do this until you train your mind to higher levels. You must fact check your thoughts before you allow them to influence your behavior and mood negatively. You can fact check your thoughts by writing them down, speaking them into a recorder, or saying them aloud and then discussing them with a trusted friend who is highly rational. You need someone who can examine your thoughts with you objectively. As an alternative, if you wish to fact check yourself privately, you may write down some of your thoughts that are bothering you. You can examine these thoughts again in a week or two, when you can look at them more objectively. This will help train you to judge whether your thoughts are accurate or not.

The bottom line here is that you should not assume that your mind is always reliable. Make your mind prove itself to you. After fact checking your thoughts and keeping a record, are you finding that your mind is assessing situations accurately, or did you waste time worrying about issues which ended up being irrelevant? Are you avoiding dangers that are not real? Are you making subjective judgments that lack support?

Remember this: To assume that all of our thoughts are rational and accurate, is itself irrational and inaccurate.

How to Avoid Becoming Chronically Negative

Do you feel that sometimes you are in a much more negative state than you would like? Perhaps you are often complaining, in a bad mood, or you have come to expect everything that you do to fail. This section will present some helpful tips for you in such cases.

Things could always be worse

It can be helpful to remind yourself that things could always be worse. The people who I have met with the worst attitudes and who complain chronically have actually had much better lives than most people. It is the people with better lives who actually have the time to complain, and the time to obsess over how their lives are not as good as someone else's – falling into the trap of comparisons. When things are truly bad, however, you don't have the time and energy to spend complaining about it.

One way to shift your perspective is to think about how people in our time have it much better than people in almost any other historic period would have had it. Most of us have medicine, modern technology, the internet, and our freedom. These are things that either did not exist in the past, or at least they were not automatically available. Almost everyone reading this book has it better than their ancestors did – what would they think if they saw you complaining over something that to them would have been trivial, perhaps even irrelevant.

We become a burden to ourselves when we start to feel sorry about our own life situation. When we sink into feeling sorry for ourselves, our challenge will be to lure out the hidden positivity from within. We may need to search deeply and use all of our might and resources, as a fisherman would, to lure a Marlin out of the sea. This is because sometimes the positivity gets hidden inside, consumed by an external cloud of negativity, but it is there, deep inside, waiting for you.

How things could always be worse

I would like you to *make a list of how things could be worse in your life*. Go ahead and make your list now, and then continue reading. I will provide my example list below so that you can compare it with yours.

- Your child could have been hurt
- You could have been fired from your job
- Your wife / husband / significant other could have left you
- Someone could have robbed you with a weapon in hand
- There could have been a major natural disaster, causing massive damage and fatalities in the area where you live
- Your home could have burned down
- This one is brutal, but someone close to you could have died suddenly

The point here is not to upset you or fill you with pessimism. The point is for you to be aware that you should feel an immense gratitude, because whatever situation you have right now, it could have been much worse.

Just be glad that...

When something goes wrong, take a deep breath, and let this thought pass through your mind:

Just be glad that...

When you back your car up and knock down your neighbor's mailbox, think *Just be glad you didn't hit a kid*. When you get fired from your job, think *Just be glad that your skills are competitive and that you should be able to find a job within 3-4 months*. When you fall off your bike and fracture your elbow, think *Just be glad that you still have one good arm you can use, and that the broken elbow will heal in time*. When you fail a class at school, think *Just be glad that you can always retake the course next semester, and this time you know to study much harder*. In the vast majority of everyday situations, there will be a silver lining, there is something good that you can choose to just be glad about.

When I was 16 years old, I made the biggest mistake of my life up to that point. It seemed like a big crisis back then, but in time I realized that it was not a problem at all. It was not the great dilemma that I imagined it to be – this is a theme you will probably find in your own life if you think back to all the crises that you have endured.

I was in my car, having recently acquired my driver's license. I wanted to make a left turn at a very busy intersection. The intersection itself was on a hill, making it difficult to see the approaching cars – especially because my car was low to the ground. Oncoming vehicles would suddenly appear, because I could not see them in the distance. I had a green light, but *not* a green arrow. According to the law, I was allowed to make a left turn with *just* the green light *if* I could judge that the path was clear. If it was not clear, I needed to wait for the green arrow.

I thought that the traffic was clear, so I proceeded with making a left turn. Unfortunately, this intersection was so big that it was taking me a very long time to complete the turn. Then, I saw a van coming toward me, but I did not have much time to react – it didn't make sense to stop in the middle of the road, so I kept going. The traffic light turned yellow. The van came closer and closer, faster and faster. Ultimately, I was hit at around 50 miles per hour by a large white van. My car was small, and it was spun around from the impact. Likely, the driver saw me in the way but did not want to slow down because the light was yellow and turning red, and she needed to get through the intersection. She was also a young driver. I believe we both made mistakes, but ultimately it was my fault for attempting to make a turn when I did not have the right of way.

My car was totaled, and the costs of repairs would have been more than the car was worth. However, I was left uninjured, without even a scratch. The other driver and her passenger were also uninjured. For several days after, I felt as if nothing could have been worse than what I did. I was highly disappointed both in my judgment and in the outcome, to say the least. But after a couple of weeks had passed, I started having thoughts like *Just be glad that you're alive.* Not only was I alive, I wasn't even cut, and I didn't break any bones, despite the massive amount of damage to the car. I also thought, *Just be glad that you didn't have a passenger in the car* – all of the impact was on that side, and anyone in that position could have been terribly injured. And I thought, *Just be glad that the car I was driving was older, and although it was a financial loss, it was not one that would cripple myself or my parents* (who actually owned the vehicle and had lent it to me).

I soon realized that there was so much to be glad about, and one of those things was actually the learning experience itself. I had become overconfident in my driving before this accident, and sometimes I was even careless, not thinking of the fact that it was incredibly important to *always* drive safely. The greater the amount of time that passed, the more I was actually grateful for this accident. It's quite possible that because I learned such a deep lesson from it, I was able to avoid having had an even worse accident through the careless habits I had been developing.

For those who have suffered through experiences that seemed horrible and unbearable, you might have also found that some of those experiences ended up bringing a lot of good in the end. It just takes time and perspective to see it.

Your mood is reflected back to you

Be aware that if you ask something in a negative mood, you will likely get a negative response and outcome. People are quite sensitive to your tone of voice, your mood, your attitude, and your body language. These are all a part of your nonverbal language. We communicate nonverbally everyday – and so you have to look for what message you are really sending to people. You may feel that you said nothing wrong to get a bad reaction, but perhaps your nonverbal communication conveyed that you were in a bad mood or in a negative state, and so people reacted defensively or irritably to you. On the other hand, if you ask something in a positive mood, you will probably get a positive response and outcome. Most of us know this, yet we still allow a bad mood to pollute our day with more and more negativity.

As an example, you can say "I need you to do this now! Stop what you're doing because that doesn't matter, and do this," in a stern and irritated tone. Or, you can say "I would appreciate it if you could help me with this right away. It is urgent, and I don't have anyone else with your expertise who can work on it. Can I count on you?" said with a pleasant, helpful attitude rather than a demanding one. The results you will get are the difference between night and day.

A theme you may find in this book is that thinking rationally helps. When you realize that you are doing something irrational, look for ways to correct that behavior through rational thinking. When you are having a bad day, think to yourself – *I know I am in a bad mood, but it only makes things worse if I have a bad attitude with everyone. I need to find it in myself to at least show a basic politeness and make the best of the situation. Perhaps through acting as if I were in a good mood, and putting a smile on my face, other people will be kind and positive in return, and that will help to put me in a better mood.*

Being negative all day will just return that negativity back to you and make things worse. It's simply rational to try to have positive interactions with the people around you.

Controlling Emotions

You are ultimately in control of yourself

Perhaps you are thinking: *But you don't understand – something always goes wrong. Of course I'm in a bad mood, but it's not my fault.*

I do not know your personal life. Of course, you may be in a very difficult situation that takes a toll on you and influences you to have a bad mood. But only you have the power to change your perceptions. And if you are unhappy or unsatisfied with what is happening around you, you also have the power to figure out solutions to change all of that.

Understand that your mind is not a machine that must produce a bad mood just because something bad happens. Some people are put in a bad mood after one bad thing happens, and some people are put in a bad mood if five bad things happen, but ultimately, you are in control of yourself. Even if ten bad things happened, you can tell yourself: *Yes, I am clearly having a bad day, but I can only control two of these things and do something about them. I will take the steps needed to fix them right away. The rest are not worth worrying about. Also, telling everyone that I know about how bad my life is won't make anything better. I should remain calm and take action instead.*

The results of out-of-control emotions

Falling into a negative, angry, bitter, or sad pattern just tends to make things worse – often much worse than they had to be. For instance, you may blow things out of proportion even when little things go wrong.

Consider this scenario:

Daniel is a manager at an office and problem after problem keeps coming up that he had not expected. Then, someone comes up to him and asks if he could pitch in $10 to buy a birthday gift for a colleague. Daniel takes out his wallet and there is no cash because he had forgotten to go to the ATM that morning. At this point, he gets angry and yells at the worker for bothering him about this when he is busy.

Daniel is so overwhelmed that any small matter seems like a dire issue, and his emotions are going out of control. We need to realize when we are confronted with many problems, that we should take a deep breath, prioritize matters, and work through them one by one calmly, in order of importance.

Continue to imagine the above scenario, where Daniel is dealing with many problems happening all at once, and someone has just asked him for cash that he did not have for the birthday gift. Then, another worker comes to him and states that she has a very important issue. She expresses in no uncertain terms that it is a critical problem that should be resolved immediately. She begins to explain how critical the issue is, and how she thinks it could be resolved. But because Daniel is already overwhelmed with other problems, he interrupts the worker and yells at her, telling her that he already has plenty of problems to deal with, and not to bother him again.

Due to Daniel's inability to put aside several normal problems and to work on the one issue that was critical, everything ended up falling apart. The worker with the critical problem tried her best to resolve it but was unable to fix it on her own. Ultimately, this was Daniel's fault, since he was the manager and she did warn him about the issue. He failed to maintain a calm composure. Instead, he made a disastrous mistake that cost the company a large number of clients, and a massive amount of income. As a result, he was fired from his job.

Understand that our own wild emotional states can make things far worse than the actual situations we have to deal with. We must learn to control our emotions and take responsibility for our actions. Claiming that we were in an emotional state and lost control is not a good explanation when you end up causing even greater problems than the original one you were faced with.

Exercising self-control

We have to learn some self-control or risk great consequences. This will be an ongoing process of learning about the self, reflecting on how and why emotions run wild, and learning to stay calm, even when situations are bad. This self-control is not gained overnight but requires a daily practice of guiding your mind to a calm, focused, self-directed place rather than allowing it to become wildly emotional based on temporary circumstances.

Remind yourself when in a tough spot:

- This is only a temporary setback
- There is a solution that will resolve this, and I just have to figure it out
- Losing control of my emotions only makes things worse – I must remain in control
- If I am not in control over myself, then who or what is in control?
- Getting angry and yelling doesn't make anyone want to help me – it just makes them want to avoid helping instead
- What are the consequences for losing emotional control? Who will I hurt and what relationships might I damage?
- It is better to take a quick break and to calm down than to try to move forward if I am feeling wildly emotional

It's difficult to remember these tips when you really need them. If you often struggle to control your emotions, write them down and keep them with you. Also, continue to add more helpful tips to your list as you learn of them.

Increase the Net Positivity in the World

Practice the Golden Rule

The *Golden Rule* states that we should treat others as we would like to be treated.

The Golden Rule is perhaps the most ubiquitous moral concept, present in many religions, cultures, and philosophies through a span of millennia. The wording is not always the same, but the same general idea appears again and again, in many different forms, throughout many periods of time.

It is in Jesus' words in the Bible (Matthew 7:12), "In everything, do to others what you would have them do to you, for this sums up the Law and the Prophets." It has been found in Buddhist teachings (Udana-Varga 5:18), "Hurt not others in ways that you yourself would find hurtful." Also, the stoic philosopher Epictetus has said similarly, "What you would avoid suffering yourself, seek not to impose on others." The principle has been found much more widely than this, as this is just a small sample of its reach.

This message of the Golden Rule is one that apparently has united much of humanity through time. It was a basic principle that most religions, philosophies and people could agree upon. Yet if we study history, it is obvious through the perpetual violence and wars that this is also something which we have struggled to put into practice.

Ask yourself: *How can I practice the Golden Rule today?*

The Tendency of Reciprocity

What I usually see in practice in our day to day lives is not the Golden Rule, but instead the *Tendency of Reciprocity*. This means that we tend to reciprocate or reflect what is done to us. If someone treats you badly, you tend to treat them badly. If someone treats you well, you tend to treat them well. This has a basic sense of justice in it, but we need to ask ourselves what is more important – is it love and togetherness, or punishment and justice? Are we going to hold a grudge and punish every action that we perceive as disagreeable? That is what the Tendency of Reciprocity would have us do.

Just as we should all seek to overcome our bad moods and bad days, we should aim to give people a pass when they are in those states. If everyone were to rush to punish me for my actions on my bad days, I would probably only become bitter, and feel that this treatment was not fully justified. Then, I would likely want to come back later and punish them for the perceived mistreatment that I received. Of course, they would feel that my treatment of them was unjustified, and so a cycle of hate, anger, and punishment would perpetuate. There has to be a better way than this. Instead of that path, if someone has their negative episode and makes a nasty remark of some kind, *learn to let it be and let it go*. As long as it is over with, you can calmly continue with your life.

All I ask is that we consider a different course of action than the Tendency of Reciprocity when someone has done something wrong. Why don't we consider the Golden Rule – doing what we would want done to us? Moreover, why don't we consider seeking out help for that person? Perhaps he is in a highly stressed state, making him behave erratically, and if someone could help to relieve his workload, or provide him help in some way, it would be enough to improve his behavior. We have to ask more questions like "How can we help someone who is being problematic?" rather than leaping straight into "How can we punish this person?"

Remember this: To spread peace and prosperity instead of anger and animosity, you must learn to let it be and let it go. Aim to lift people up, rather than to tear them down and fuel the fury within them.

Random acts of kindness & pay it forward

Look for opportunities to do something kind, even if there is no particular reason for it. You can also practice *paying it forward* – which is to do something kind for a *different person* after someone has done something kind for you. But I see no point in waiting. You are always capable of making someone's day just a bit brighter by doing something nice right now. I would encourage you to perform an act of kindness regularly. If you stick to very small acts, you could even do this on a daily basis. For example, you could smile at a stranger. You would be surprised at the impact it can make.

Here are some ideas of random acts of kindness that you can perform:

- Pay for someone's coffee
- Compliment someone's eyes, smile, laugh, etc.
- Help someone lift something heavy
- Give to a homeless person – it doesn't have to be money, it could be food, clothing, or even conversation
- Tutor or babysit without pay
- Offer to help someone through a crisis – offer something specific such as to pick up groceries
- Provide company for someone who is lonely, or for an elderly person
- If you are interested in a deeper way to make an impact, you may volunteer at an organization that helps people

Make everything better than it was when you found it

This idea is just a reminder to generally be more considerate of the spaces you occupy and in everything you do. If you remember to leave things better than you found them, you will always be in a mode that is considerate of others. When you visit and dine with someone, you will remember to offer to help clean up. When you are in a public park, you will remember not to litter. If you borrow an item such as a book from someone, you will remember to take good care of it. This level of consideration will help remind you to keep your environment positive. Many of us forget this type of consideration because we don't always see the effects of our actions. If someone has to clean up, it often happens when we have already left. If you had to sit and watch someone clean up after you, perhaps you would feel embarrassed and realize that you should have helped with this. Even in a relationship, you should seek to help your partner to improve and become better, not to drain or contribute to his or her stress and agony day after day. Aim to make everything better through your presence.

Turn your Superpain into your Superpower

If you are in immense pain from some great tragedy that has happened in your life, you may not know how to manage that pain or what to do with it. You may find that it controls you and takes a hold of your life, and you may feel that there is not much you can do to move forward. The immense pain may have left you feeling as if there were a void inside of you. Whenever you are ready, however, there is a path forward, which has been carried out by many prominent people. Understand that tremendous pain and the dark energy that surrounds it can ultimately be transformed into positive energy, a force for good.

If you have ever known someone who was *too* good at their work, or at their mission, or even at being a parent, people such as this have often overcome a great pain in their past. They are motivated not by a paycheck or a simple reward, but by a tremendous force inside of them which feels a need to overcome a dark past filled with pain, and the way to do that is to replace the bad with the good. They are busy converting painful energies into positive and productive energies, because they have come to understand that this is the path forward, so as not to allow the darkness to overcome them. Doing nothing is not an option, because the pain would then overwhelm them. Ultimately, these people have turned their *Superpain* into their *Superpower*.

I would never encourage anyone to seek out immense pain in their lives. But sometimes the pain chooses us, and the only option we have is to drown in our miseries, or to turn the pain into something positive for ourselves and for others. Of course, the first one is not a real option. Rather, we should choose the second one. In the process of living out our superpowers, we will create a healing feeling inside. In time, the pain from within can be healed or repaired through positive action.

See the stories below for examples of people who turned their Superpain into their Superpower.

John Walsh and his family

John Walsh is famously known for hosting the longest running crime reality show in Fox's history, *America's Most Wanted*. He and the show aided in the capture of more than 1,000 fugitives.

John Walsh isn't just an ordinary man who wanted to stop criminals from getting away with their crimes. Something horrific happened in his life that made him want to make a difference, to help prevent others from having to suffer like he and his family did.

On July 27th, 1981, in the middle of the day, his wife Revé took their son Adam to a Sears store. The boy was six years old and he went to watch some boys play on a video game display while his mother was looking for a lamp to buy. When she came back about five minutes later, he was gone. Of course, she and staff members searched for him, but they could not find Adam anywhere. Ultimately, search parties and helicopters were dispatched to help find the boy, but they could not find him either. A few weeks later, the unthinkable happened. Adam Walsh's severed head was found in a drainage canal, 140 miles north of the Walsh's home. The body was never found.

Obviously, this must be the most horrific ordeal that any parent could possibly have to endure. But instead of allowing this nightmare to destroy them, the Walsh family decided to make a difference. John Walsh dedicated his life to searching for criminals, and to help prevent anything like this from ever happening again, especially to a child. He and his wife were involved in various initiatives to help missing and exploited children and other victims. For example, the Walsh family founded the Adam Walsh Child Resource Center, a non-profit organization dedicated to making better laws with the aim of reducing the amount of child victims. Also, their activism helped for Code Adam to be implemented in department stores. A Code Adam was announced when a child would go missing in a store, and procedures were put in place to help find the child quickly and to keep him safe.

Through the efforts of John Walsh and his family, they have aided countless children from becoming victims. They have dedicated their lives to extinguishing evil forces in this world, and to keep our children safe so that they could live out the bright future that awaits them.

Oprah Winfrey

At just three years old, Oprah was taught to read by her grandmother, Hattie Mae. When she was supposed to start kindergarten, she wrote a letter to her teacher saying that she belonged in the first grade. She was moved on to the first grade promptly, and then she skipped second grade to attend the third grade.

At such an early age, her future appeared to be so bright. However, things would soon change….

During her Australian tour in 2015, she stated: "I was raped at nine years old by a cousin, then again by another family member, and another family member."

By 14 years old, as a result of sexual abuse, she became pregnant. She was so distraught with her situation that she hid the fact that she was pregnant from her family and she thought about suicide. Oprah ended up going into labor prematurely, although tragically, her baby boy died in the hospital just two weeks later. She was only 14 years old and had already suffered the loss of a child. She never even had the chance to hold the baby, and the baby was not given a name (although as recently as 2015, she did name him Canaan).

This could have been the last that we ever heard about Oprah. It would be easy to believe that from this point on, the person discussed above could have easily gone down a dark road, failing to live up to her potential. Instead, we have someone who has led a hugely successful career, with the highest rated talk show in American television history, *The Oprah Winfrey Show*. She is also someone who has given immensely to charities and who has given her words of wisdom freely.

In my view, Oprah used her immense pain to better understand other people, and to help them so that they would not have to go through the level of pain that she went through as a child. She did what she could to help people or even to save them, as she herself wished she could have been saved.

As a powerful lesson on how our pain can ultimately give us greater meaning than the perfect life that we would wish for, consider what Oprah has told *The Weekly*: "Had I been born in a family where I felt nurtured, supported or loved, I would not be where I am today. I would have had far less need to prove that I was worthy of space in the world."

Jane McGonigal

Jane McGonigal is an American game designer who aims to build games that can help improve the quality of human lives. Among her many accomplishments, she has been recognized as one of the "20 Most Inspiring Women in the World" by Oprah Winfrey for *O Magazine* and as one of the "Top 35 innovators changing the world through technology" by the *MIT Technology Review*.

As discussed in her book, *SuperBetter*, in the summer of 2009 she suffered through a concussion which didn't heal properly. As a result of the injury, she was forced to endure a slow recovery period where she was unable to do the things she loved – reading, writing, playing video games, and so on. At some point, her mind was telling her that the pain would never end, and she was in agony both from the symptoms of the concussion, and from her own negative thinking. At her lowest point, she decided "I am either going to kill myself, or I am going to turn this into a game."

Fortunately, she did make a game called *Jane the Concussion Slayer*, where the purpose was to heal her brain. The first person she played this game with was her twin sister. Together, they battled *bad guys*, which were things that would trigger her symptoms, such as bright lights and crowded spaces. They also pursued *power-ups* for Jane, which were things that could help her to feel better or productive, even if only slightly, due to her injury. An example would be getting out of bed and walking around the block just once.

Jane's fog of depression and anxiety lifted after a couple of days. Her pain didn't end so fast, but her mental anguish and feelings of hopelessness did. Ultimately, she created a game that others could play, called SuperBetter (which is also the title of her book).

From her great pain, she discovered that playing games could help in the recovery process, and she wanted to share this discovery by making her own game to help other people who were also suffering. Thus far, SuperBetter has helped around a half million people to cope with illnesses such as depression, anxiety, chronic pain, and traumatic brain injuries.

In the above cases, we have dramatic accounts of people who successfully turned their Superpain into their Superpower. The people above, and anyone else who has followed such a path, all deserve our great respect and admiration. I hope if you are in deep pain, or if you go through a deep pain at some point, that you are able to convert that painful energy into something that can be for the greater good.

Remember this:

Every moment of your life is an opportunity for failure which leads to learning, knowledge which leads to understanding, wrongdoing which leads to redemption, suffering which leads to healing, your foes to become friends, your source of weakness to become your source of strength, your Superpain to become your Superpower, and love to overcome fear.

The beautiful thing about humanity is we are capable of transforming evil, wrongs, pain, and suffering into something that is positive, noble, heroic, and good. The challenge is realizing that we are capable of this, and then actually doing it.

A Caveat to Positive Thinking

Understand that some situations can make it overwhelmingly difficult to practice positive thinking. In some places, such as in a bad environment or perhaps a bad neighborhood, virtually everyone around you may have a negative attitude and persona. This tends to be a defense mechanism to shield people when they are aware that they are in a highly negative place. Perhaps violence, scams, drug use, and lack of respect are common in the area, and so people learn to adopt a negative attitude to protect themselves. A negative attitude tells everyone– *leave me alone, I'm not the person you want to target.* In this world, someone who is open to new experiences and in a good mood becomes the obvious target for all of the negativity. Whoever is doing well is someone that everyone else wants to bring down, however they can. Of course, in such cases, do what you must for your survival, but inside your mind you must maintain control and stay positive.

When you are surrounded by negativity and toxicity, it is more important than ever that you develop a positive mindset. The environment will try to drag you down. People may act as if nothing matters, as if aspiring for greatness or working hard is futile, and as if you and everyone they know are worthless. They may act as if life is irrelevant and dying young is no big deal. Some of these people may think that today is the only day to live for – in a destructive, self-limiting way, not in a conscious and present way. Ultimately, they may live a life of misdeeds and of sabotaging others.

When your situation involves some or all of these attitudes, you must develop an internal positivity that is unshakeable. One of the best things that you can do is to cautiously distance yourself from others if they have become dragged down into the negative environment. For family members, you may try to get them to understand that this negative mindset is problematic. But for other people in your life, just let it go. Standing out too much from the crowd could get you into trouble in such a place.

When you are in an environment where doing bad things is actually viewed as good, and doing good things is viewed as bad, you have to be cautious. You should consider keeping a low profile, and distancing yourself from what is going on around you. Instead, you may quietly save your money to move to a better place. Or you could spend your time reading, to build knowledge and skills that can help you to get ahead. Consider free resources such as what may be available at a public library. Another option is to seek to network with potential mentors – you can seek them out online if you are unsure of where to begin.

To keep an internal positive state, you will need to minimize the external negativity as much as you can. Unfortunately, you may be forced into isolating yourself from others just to shield yourself from the negativity, but as you move away from it, some positive people may become attracted to you. If you find a few good friends that you can trust, this may be all that you need.

Exercises

Create a Positivity Box (the opposite of a Pandora's Box)

Your *Positivity Box* could be an actual box, or it could just be a journal, notebook, or scrapbook (physical or digital) that contains quotes, music, videos, pictures, and general reminders of things that are positive in life. You may include a quote by Oprah Winfrey such as: "Surround yourself only with people who are going to take you higher." You may have the song *Happy*, sung by Pharrell Williams, or a card written by your child. Alternatively, you could include a list of everything you are grateful for. Another option is to include photos that record positive memories with family and friends. Any time you struggle to stay positive, open your Positivity Box, and remind yourself of all that is good in the world.

Count your positive and negative thoughts

Set an alarm to go off at the top of every hour for a day, and log what you were thinking about at the time. Write one line about what you were thinking, and also write if it was positive, neutral, or negative. If you mostly had negative thoughts, then this is a dangerous path that needs to be corrected. If you mostly had positive thoughts, then that is good. If you were in the middle, then you could benefit from more positivity in your life. Aim to always have more positive thoughts than negative ones – preferably much more.

Start and end with something positive

Start and end your days like this: Think about what is going right, what is good, and what you are grateful for – it can also be helpful to write this down. Or if you are big on consuming news and media, start and end your days by consuming a positive piece of media and sharing it with others. Consider positive news outlets such as *Good News Network*, *Sunny Skyz*, and *Daily Good*.

See yourself in a positive light by flipping your negative traits into positive ones

Take everything that is negative about yourself and flip it into a positive trait. Whenever someone tells you that you are the negative trait, flip it and tell them that you are actually the positive one. For example, you are not stubborn, you are persevering. You are not lazy, you use your resources efficiently. You are not ignorant, you are open to learning new things.

Use your words for good

Think of a time when you used your words to spread anger, hate, fear, or pain. Even if you don't know how someone reacted to what you said, imagine how they may have reacted. The point of this is not to make you feel bad. We all say things that we shouldn't have sometimes. Instead, the point is to get you to reflect, so that you realize the power of your words to hurt others, and so that you are more cautious with this in the future. The next time you are tempted to use your words in a dark way, use them for good instead.

Do a random act of kindness

If you need an idea for something to do, then compliment an adult. Adults are rarely complimented and are starving for such positive attention. You will find that giving a genuine compliment to someone can feel good both for you and the receiver. Otherwise you can smile at a stranger, or offer to help someone with an errand instead of waiting for this person to ask. Another fun thing to do is to give someone an unexpected gift.

Get physical exercise

Getting physical exercise can often help you get away from your problems and to clear your mind so that you can start fresh and see things in a more positive light. For bonus points, if you are in good shape, engage in exercise that is physically demanding, to help relieve yourself from a mind that is dwelling on the negative.

THOUGHT #3

Focus on What You Can Do, *Not* on What You Cannot Do

"If you can't fly then run, if you can't run then walk, if you can't walk then crawl, but whatever you do you have to keep moving forward."
— Martin Luther King, Jr.

Moving Beyond *Just* Positive Thinking

As we know, positive thinking on its own is not enough to solve the problems that come up in our everyday lives. Living in a bubble of positive thinking will not change the negative realities around you. Sometimes things are bad and we have to do something about it. For such situations, we move on to this Thought, which is based on taking action instead of staying stuck in thought.

Focusing on what you can do will become more important when you face a problem. Often, we view problems as something negative in our lives, but they are natural, and there will always be new ones for us to face. It doesn't help to see the problems themselves as a great negative force in our lives — if we see them this way, we will often feel overwhelmed and drained, wondering why we have so many. I prefer to have the approach that problems are placed in front of me so that I can become a better problem-solver and so that I can become mentally more tough. Problems and obstacles do not exist to defeat us. We are meant to overcome them. Really, we should see them as *opportunities*, and not as *problems*.

Keep in mind that we humans make problems every day, as we are the world's best problem-makers. Fortunately, we are also the world's best problem-solvers – we can solve them, overcome them, and even make them *poof* – vanish, if we want to. Often times, things happen in life that we do not like. To nature or the animal, this is just life. To the human, we perceive this as a problem that needs to be fixed. See everything as a problem to be fixed and live life that way, or see things as being just as they were meant to be and live life that way. The choice is yours.

One way that we create problems for ourselves is that when an issue presents itself, we tend to focus on the things we cannot do, and on the reasons that the issue cannot be resolved. Here are some examples of such thought processes:

We don't have the right tool to make progress on building something.

We can't make progress on this because our expert colleague is out of town.

If we proceed in this way the boss will get mad and we will get in trouble.

We naturally tend to find the worlds of possibilities of what we cannot do, of what cannot be done, without stopping to propose solutions. Understand that the mind tends to be creative for all that is wrong – we find reasons that we can't, instead of reasons that we can. It is our task to train the mind to be creative for all that is good, so that we can begin to find solutions.

The brain may have infinite potential in terms of what we can accomplish with it. But in order to reach such states, we have to know how to properly use it. If you waste your brain power in processing what you cannot do, how will you ever figure out what you can do? When we face many problems, or difficult problems, we tend to fall into negative thinking states, but it is critical that we stay positive, as this will help us to keep focus on what we are capable of doing to improve the situation. It doesn't make sense to sit around, feeling bad about your inability to do something. You need to make the conscious choice to make progress.

When facing a problem or some kind of issue, ask yourself: *What can I do to solve this? Who can help me with this? What tools do I need to resolve this? What information do I need and where can I access it?*

Sometimes, when you are overwhelmed, a simple way to clear the mind is to ask: *What is the first step I need to take?*

This simple question has a way of clearing the mind so that you can focus on what you must do next. It's easy to get caught up in too many things that you need to do. If you can slow the mind down to focus on the next action that you must take, then your job will be much easier.

Just as we all have infinite things that we can't do, which we could focus on, we also have an infinite number of things that we can do, if we would just focus on that. Pointing out what you can't do doesn't help you to move forward. It keeps you static, in a state of complaint, in a frozen bubble where the world is moving forward but you are standing still. Actually, you are moving backward, because if everyone else is moving forward then you are falling behind. This is the price of over-focusing on the *can'ts* of your life.

The Self-Fulfilling Prophecy: Whatever You Believe Will Probably Come True

Have you ever labeled someone or been labeled by someone? By labeling someone as *selfish*, *bad with money*, *stupid*, etc., we are actually giving them permission to be these things. By believing that they are these things, we will set them up to fulfill these roles. Whether we expect them to succeed or fail, we are guiding them toward what we expect to happen. Be cautious with what you expect from yourself and others – it is likely to come true.

Think of how we use labels in society. Criminals are "convicts" and "ex-convicts", instead of "citizens in need of redemption" and "redeemed". We restrict what people feel they are capable of doing when we label them. A label is a constricting device, that narrows the paths that you feel are available to you. If we must label, we need to be careful to use them for good instead of for bad.

When I was a child, I was labeled as a *troublemaker* by teachers for a few years. I remember sometimes thinking that if I wanted to do something and it was wrong, that I might as well do it. I was just fulfilling a role that was set out for me. I also noticed that when I did something wrong, the teachers may not be surprised, or may even say something like "I knew it had to be you." They were so sure that I was involved with any trouble, that it only made sense to me to live out *their* expectations. In my heart, I knew that I was not a troublemaker, but the power of their expectation had a greater effect on me than my personal will, at that age. Luckily, I outgrew this role by around ten years old.

The point for us to understand is that even as adults, we are often given roles and it can be very difficult to overcome them. The sad truth is that much of the time we are not who we are, but who we are expected to be. Expect greatness from yourself and others, and you just may get it. If you have been given a role of failure, wrongness, and stupidity, then you are much more likely to live out this role.

Do not accept all of the roles that people want to give you. Choose them wisely for yourself.

For any negative labels that you place on yourself or that others place on you, you must unshackle yourself from them. Write down any negative labels used on you and remake them to present you in a more positive, limitless light. This will help you to see that you are not truly defined in a negative way. For instance, "troublemaker" is a tough one, but how about "opportunistic activity finder" – after all, that is what troublemakers are in school – kids who find things to do that don't relate to the defined curriculum. It only took me five seconds to think of this, so don't stop looking even if you think that you have a tough label to overcome.

To Conform or Not Conform

Don't conform or go against what others are doing as an automatic course of action. Think things through. You have free will. You do not need to agree with and follow everything that someone says or does, of course. But you also do not need to be defined by your family, your neighborhood, or your country. You do not need to be defined by their beliefs (especially limiting ones), their politics, their habits, the things they choose to focus on, or their goals. You are allowed to have your own independent thoughts which do not follow the conventional patterns. You have to give yourself permission to think for yourself, or it may not happen. When you sense yourself losing your free will, tell yourself: *I give myself permission to think for myself, and to take action based on what I think.*

On the contrary, some of us have a strong inner rebel that drives us to disagree and to go against the general opinions automatically, and this is also a mistake. This rebellious side wishes to show others that we are in control, and that we can freely disagree or go against the crowds. This is supposed to prove our free will, but it does not. If you always go against the crowds without thought, then you are not really free. You are just as mindless as anyone who always conforms without thought. This urge to not conform, or to do the opposite of what others are doing or suggesting, has a name in the psychological literature – *reactance bias.*

Be aware that if you are too rebellious and nonconforming, you will be easily manipulated by others – as they can expect that any request or suggestion will be met with your opposition. All they need to do is request that you do the opposite of what they actually want you to do, employing *reverse psychology.*

My recommendation is to peacefully detach yourself from both options. Do not conform blindly, and do not disagree with the prevailing thoughts blindly. Find the third path where you do not feel restrained by either going with the conforming path or the nonconforming one. You are able to make your own choice based on independent thinking. Make your choice because it is you and because it is right, not because you are being guided toward or away from something.

Problem-Solving

The following are some tips for how to go about solving everyday problems that arise.

Keep a positive, calm mindset

When you meet a lot of resistance and you feel yourself getting frustrated, take a breath, take a break, take a walk, and get a different perspective on the problem from someone else. If you allow a negative spiral of thoughts, you make things worse. Tasks that should be easy can become difficult quite quickly. You stop thinking clearly, which can cause you to make mistake after mistake. Sometimes it is best to do nothing, to leave the problem alone and then to come back when you feel fresh and ready to tackle it.

I have observed many times that when people are in a rush to force a solution, and they are impatient, this is a time when errors are more likely to occur. Also, there are many times when people get frustrated because they are thinking of the problem in one way, but if they were to calm themselves and see it with fresh eyes, they would see that the solution is quite simple. Ask yourself if you are overcomplicating things. Perhaps there is a simpler way to accomplish what you would like to do. For example, can you add something, remove something, or change the order of certain actions?

Information gathering

To solve any problem you will need to have the right information. If you do not already have the information that you need to arrive at a good decision, then the first thing you must do is gather the information that you will need.

It is easy to fall into the trap of agonizing when you don't have the right information. Because you don't have this information, you assume that it will be difficult to find, and that it will be difficult to apply. I sometimes find that I am dreading doing a task that I don't know how to start. Then when I seek out the relevant information, I realize that it is actually much easier and takes much less time than I would have expected. Sure, some tasks are more difficult and will take longer, but what I have said here is quite logical when you think of it. If you are dreading something because you have built it up in your mind, then there is a good chance that the actual task will not be as bad as you expected. Your mind has made it worse than it actually had to be. Be aware that it is easy to feel overwhelmed when you don't know where to begin, but that after finding the necessary information, you are likely to feel relieved, focused, and prepared to take action.

To find the relevant information for your problem, you may look up information online, talk to people with experience, or read books. Often, with complex problems you are not alone. Either a superior will know how to help you get started, or possibly a colleague or friend. Consider who is likely to have had a similar problem – and you may ask such a person where you can begin to find the information that you need to resolve it. In some cases, there are specific organizations or services built around helping you with certain tasks, or to help you answer questions on a specific topic. Be sure to consider such options as well. Remember that when you have the right information, everything else becomes easier.

Write down all of your options

When you have gathered the information that you need, you should discover what your options are. If there is not one clear path to pursue, write down all of your options.

Identify your best options and necessary tasks

Next, identify the best options, and the ones that are absolutely necessary for you to perform. Eliminate the ones that are not practical or that are not good options. Perhaps they would cost too much time or money, or you are not sure that they would work.

Organize a list of steps to perform

From all of your options, organize a list of steps that you can take to resolve the problem. This will be your action plan that you can implement. If there is a good backup option, then write that down too, so if your main plan does not work you can always go with the backup option.

Take the first step

Take the first step in your action plan and continue following your steps until you have implemented your plan fully. If at any point you are not comfortable with proceeding on your own, you should find someone with more experience with your problem who can help guide you.

"Do or do not. There is no try." – Yoda from Star Wars: Episode V - The Empire Strikes Back

I sometimes catch myself and other people using the word "try," which is a bad start in focusing on what you *can* do. If you find yourself saying "try," you should force yourself to make an action plan (e.g., a list of steps to follow) and to bring your focus onto what you *will* do. "Try" is a word that we use when we are ready to fail – it puts us in the wrong frame of mind. We don't think that we can do something, so we use that word. We say: "I'm going to *try* to study harder." "I'm going to *try* to lose weight." "I'm going to *try* to find a better job." None of these identifies a clear plan of action, and so none of these "tries" is likely to succeed.

Some "tries" are ridiculous when you think of them. Sometimes I hear novice writers say, "I'm going to try to write." Well, if you are going to write something down on a sheet of paper or on your computer, then this isn't called *trying to write*. That is called *writing*.

Be careful of such thinking – often, we use the word "try" when we are scared to work on something, fearing that we may not succeed immediately. I have to ask – why must we always succeed immediately? Why must everything always work out perfectly? We need to manage our expectations so that we are not so scared of small failures that we can't even begin a task.

I would urge you to *not* turn this Thought into *I will focus on what I can try to do*. Make sure that it stays *I will focus on what I can do*. From there, list out your options, formulate a plan, and then *focus on what you will do*.

Remember this: Stop trying and start doing.

More Options are Not Always Better

When there are an excessive amount of available options, I find that I am much happier when I limit the choices for myself. Looking for the best option doesn't always make people happy because when there are too many of them, they end up wondering later if they chose the best one. Also, I do not enjoy the process of searching for the best option, when most of the options available are already good. In such cases, I will limit the selection quickly. This is much better than feeling the need to look through every option and to weigh it against every other option, as this can be quite time-consuming and ultimately most products are usually good enough for what I need.

Of course, for major life decisions, it can be well worth it to investigate your options thoroughly – which college to go to, which house to buy, which jobs to apply to. However, even there, you may be happier when you set your own limits. You only want to go to a college in your state perhaps, or that has a good reputation in engineering, or you only want to buy a house that is in one of three excellent neighborhoods, or you will only apply to jobs in the northeast region of your country.

Be willing to spend more time investigating all of your options on major life decisions, but if you feel overwhelmed or anxious by making everyday life choices, then look for ways to limit your options to something reasonable. I will attempt to limit my options to just 2 or 3 as quickly as I can for basic everyday choices, such as choosing something on a menu or toothpaste or which cinema to go to. If I'm truly unhappy with the selection, I will find 2-3 more options until I'm satisfied. For major life decisions, I may seek out 10-15 options, and if I am not fully happy, to once again seek 10-15 more options to look through. This allows you to spend more time living a good life, and less time trying to make the perfect choice.

Your Comfort Zone Affects What You Can Do

How comfortable are you right now? Probably comfortable enough, as you are reading a book. But hopefully in your life, you are not *too* comfortable. Allow me to explain.

For those of us who seek comfort, we have to be careful. If you make no plan to change anything in your life, then your comfort zone will be in a natural state of constant restriction, restricting what you can do, and increasing the size of what you cannot do. At least, it restricts your mind into believing this. The mind then restricts the body.

I have had personal experience with this constricting comfort zone. In the past I used to have a bad habit of seeking more and more comfort, which in the end just led to misery. By moving away from things that made me uncomfortable, I believed that I would feel more comfortable – this seems reasonable, but it doesn't work this way. In fact, through seeking comfort, I was starting to become phobic of everything. The zone of comfort was closing tight around me like a noose and I was starting to understand how people could develop many psychological disorders – phobias such as agoraphobia, anxiety disorders, a lifelong crippling depression, etc.

There was a point where I didn't want to do anything new. I was essentially neophobic (e.g., afraid of new things), talking myself out of doing anything new that could make me uncomfortable. The idea of doing something new gave me anxiety rather than a feeling of excitement.

Instead of going down that dark path, it is important to challenge yourself regularly so that you do not get too comfortable. Then, life's little difficulties become a form of excitement, and not something that you need to fear or worry about. In time, you become much better prepared for life's big challenges too.

Larry Page, co-founder and CEO of Google has said "Always work hard on something uncomfortably exciting." This quote seems to focus on work, but the idea is so powerful that we should expand it into our everyday lives. Do one thing that uncomfortably excites you every day. At least do it once a week if that is all that you can do. It needs to become a habit so that you can always be moving forward, expanding the situations in which you feel energized. This doesn't mean that you need to say "Yes" to every new thing that comes your way. But become alert if you find yourself saying "No" to every new opportunity, and often just because it might make you feel uncomfortable. That is a warning sign that you must change.

Make Your "To-Don't List": Not Everything You Can Do is Something You Should Do

The point in focusing on what you can do is that many of us waste time, life, and energy worrying about the things we cannot do. Instead, we should focus on the world of possibilities that are available to us. This is the way to move forward with our lives and avoid feeling stuck.

However, as I'm sure you have seen in your life – just because you can do something, doesn't mean that you should do it. What we should *not* do is probably as important as what we *can* do. When you realize that you are doing something bad for you, and that you aren't getting anything positive from it, this would be a good action to add to your *To-Don't list*. Just as many people keep To-Do lists, I would advise you to create your To-Don't list. Simply write down the things in your life that are not worth doing – they waste your time, they waste your energy, they make you feel miserable, and they are inefficient.

Of course, it is not easy to completely remove all bad habits and actions that are not useful from your life. But bringing them into awareness and putting them onto a list can be a good start. If you don't identify a problem, it will never be fixed.

Here is an example of how to limit a bad behavior. I like to play games, but if I play too many games, I find that I lose motivation for my work and it is no longer a positive aspect of my life. Thus, my To-Don't list includes *not to play games more than two hours per day*. Usually, I do not play more than about an hour a day, but two hours is the hard limit that I set for myself. The point here is that your To-Don't list doesn't need to be a firm list telling you 100% not to do something. I enjoy games and I would like to always keep them in my life, but I realize that too much of anything can be bad for you. Your To-Don't list is a good place to set limits on the tasks that work against your own best interests.

If you have tried to stop something that you know is bad for you, but you could not get rid of the habit "cold turkey" or with the available programs that exist, you may plan to gradually reduce the behavior. For instance, if you normally smoke 3-4 cigarettes a day, you could set a limit of 2 per day. This doesn't solve the problem, certainly, but it brings you closer to your goal without setting unreasonable expectations on yourself. People tend to get used to a new level of normal in time. If smoking 3-4 cigarettes is normal for you now, you can retrain yourself to perceive 2 cigarettes as normal with some dedication. Then you can ease your way down to one, then to none. The trick is to do it so slowly that your brain perceives it all as normal.

Remember that diets and programs to overcome addictions often don't work, perhaps because they are too radical and ambitious. If that approach works for you, great, but for the rest of us, we may need a more gradual approach.

Make the Impossible Possible

Just because something has not been done does not mean that it cannot be done. Be careful not to limit your range of what you can do. Don't assume that you can't do something, for generally we are capable of much more than we would think. We live in an age of great technology with an abundance of informational resources, where I believe that practically anyone could achieve what they can envision, given enough time, willpower, and resources. Of course, it is not easy. Many ambitious visions will require a highly dedicated team, and plenty of funds to pay them and to invest in creating something worthwhile. However, I believe that if your ideas are great enough, you will attract the right teams and the right funds. If you lack access to this, then spend your time educating yourself, learning everything about your field technically, and building great ideas. Then, when you meet the right person who could open doors for you, you can clearly show that you have a vision and that you have a plan that can work.

Don't feel too strongly that anything is impossible. If you go back far enough in time, everything that we do today appears to be impossible. What people say is impossible today becomes possible to do tomorrow.

Keep in mind that if you want something to work and you search hard enough, you can often find a way to make it happen. As long as you are not tied down to one way of doing things, you can find a way to get the outcome you wanted. While it may be true that one particular action that you would like to take could not work, there may be a hundred other actions you could take that would get you the right result.

For instance, according to the Edison Museum, Thomas Edison and his assistants tested over 6,000 filaments while searching for a filament that was long-lasting and cheap. It's easy to imagine that after those first 6,000 tries, someone could have told Edison that this will never work. They could have advised him to give up, because it seemed like he and his workers were wasting their time. Of course, Edison would not give up so easily, because the idea of getting cheap light to many people was so important. And someone persistent enough to try 6,000 filaments may have been willing to continue no matter what.

The point to understand here is that the statement, "These 6,000 filaments will not produce a long-lasting and cheap lightbulb," would have been true. But the statement, "We cannot produce a long-lasting lightbulb," would have been untrue. Don't give up, because even if the action does not work immediately, there is often another way to arrive at the outcome that you desired.

Sometimes, people will tell us that we can't do something. That we're not good enough, and that we'll never be good enough. What do we do then? Should we give up?

It is always possible that people are telling you that you can't do something because they can't do it themselves, and so they prefer to see you fail so that you cannot be better than them. Or perhaps they want to protect you from a high probability of failure – which is reasonable to expect, if no one else has succeeded at something you are attempting to do. Another reason you may be told that you can't do something is that an expert actually believes you are not good enough, based on her experience. However, this expert may just want to test you, to see if you have the drive to persist in the face of challenges. And sometimes, you will be misjudged. An expert may think you are not willing to put in the work and that you are not skilled enough. But even the experts can be wrong.

Remember that people are often quite short-sighted. If someone tells you that you can't do something, usually what they mean is that you can't do it yet. If you're not ready, then get ready and come back to your task when you are prepared. And of course, if you decide that a task is not what you really want to do, you are always able to leave and do something else. There are always options. Abandoning a path that was not working for you does not make you a failure.

Understand that we are naturally limited based on what we have seen and experienced. If you said that you wanted to take humans to the moon in the year 1500, no one would even have comprehended that possibility. But fast forward to the 1960s, and people understood that it may be possible with the quick advancements of technology. Of course, Americans did land on the moon in 1969. If you propose something that no one has seen and they can't understand how you could get there, they will tell you that you can't do it. But with enough persistence and dedication, perhaps you can get there. If nothing else, you can dedicate yourself to the pursuit of creating the conditions that will make something possible. It may be true that something is not immediately possible. But when you have an impossible dream or mission, you must ask yourself: *What is the first step I must take to make this possible.*

Forget What We Typically Think of as Perfection

The pursuit of perfection is a fantasy that causes people much grief. This is a pursuit that is admirable yet misguided.

Life is like a work of performance art, or like a theater play if you prefer. Regardless of what happens, the show must go on. If you forget your lines, or what you had planned to say, or what you were supposed to do, you must still continue. The true perfection instead is to master this ability to press on, to move forward despite the imperfect circumstances that we find ourselves in. The true perfection is to craft yourself as a work of art, creating what you need and want yourself to be, and becoming fluid and adaptable, able to work with whatever circumstances life may hand you. The true perfection is to accept your imperfections and to *do your best*.

Seeking perfection takes you further away from it, because you will always be upset at not attaining it, and this will hurt your performance. Keeping this in mind, I would advise you to *forget the need for perfection*.

Instead, just *do the best you can* with:

What you have (See Thought #4) – what resources do you have at your disposal? This can be people, things, money, your own intellectual and creative abilities, books, etc.

What you know – think about your knowledge, skills, and abilities. What are you capable of doing? Is there something you've overlooked? Do people often notice a strength in you that you have never paid much attention to?

The options or choices you have – Don't just stop at the first few obvious options. You may be surprised to find that there are many other options available that you haven't thought of. What if you change the order that you typically perform certain actions in? What if you seek outside help? What if you take a break from thinking about it, then come back to it later? Or what if you did nothing? As strange as it seems, sometimes doing nothing is the best option. If every option available to you is likely to cause more harm or problems than doing nothing, then perhaps you should do nothing.

The information that you are able to look up – Do you have books, access to the internet and a search engine, a library, or research articles? Often, we place the burden of figuring out a problem on ourselves. But most problems we face have also been faced by someone else. If we could simply look up how the problem has been solved in the past, then we could solve it for ourselves too.

Any knowledgeable contacts that you may have – When you don't know how to make progress yourself, seek out people who can help you. Remember, even if your personal network is small, you can always look up experts online. I would encourage you to find such experts and ask them a question if you think that they could be of help. Be concise, explain the problem clearly, and tell them what you have done to try to solve it. Of course, you should have tried many other options before doing this. I believe most experts are willing to help, but they will likely be annoyed if you ask a basic question that is easily searchable online.

Your abilities (e.g., to be logical, reasonable, intuitive, and creative) – You are your own greatest resource. Tony Robbins, the world-renowned motivational speaker has said that your resourcefulness is your greatest resource. In his seminars, he has said: "Creativity, decisiveness, passion, honesty, sincerity, love, these are the ultimate human resources. And when you engage these resources, you can get any other resource on Earth."

What this means is that when you lack resources, this is an opportunity to see how resourceful you can be. How many creative ideas can you come up with to resolve a problem only with the items currently at your disposal? How honest and straightforward can you be with someone to make them realize the importance of your problem? How passionate can you be to attract people to your cause? How loving can you be to make other people see that you are just as worthy as they themselves are? Use your ultimate resources to attract any other resource that you need.

The given moment – train yourself to *not* get stuck thinking about a better situation you might have had in a prior moment. Often in life, when we had a better situation in the past, we regret our mistakes and dwell on them, wondering what we did wrong. Really, we should learn to quickly rebound from mistakes, so that we can focus fully on making the best of the present opportunities in front of us (See Thought #5). Or if there aren't any opportunities readily available, then we should find ways to create them. If you allow yourself to become disheartened and focused on what went wrong, then you are likely to make more mistakes in your bitterness. By clinging to what was, you will be heading in the wrong direction. We must learn to control the mind, because otherwise we can get stuck in harmful patterns.

Remember this: Do the best you can with what you have, what you know, your options, the information and knowledge you have, your abilities, and the given moment. If you are doing your best, no one can expect anything more from you.

Exercises

Do something that makes you *uncomfortably excited*

Get a sheet of paper and list out all of the things that would make you uncomfortably excited. This may involve travels such as visiting a place you always wanted to go to but that you never found the time for. It may involve pursuing a new relationship or friendship. This could involve a great challenge that you have been worried about pursuing, because you did not want to fail. Perhaps someone has recently presented you with an opportunity that deep down you wanted to do, but you were worried and so you turned it down – you may choose to pursue this opportunity, or a new one similar to it.

Write down all of your areas of expertise

What are you knowledgeable in? What are your skills and abilities? Write down all that you are capable of doing. Having such a list is useful for times when you are feeling hopeless, and like you have no options available to you. Whenever you feel limited, take out this list and remind yourself of all that you are able to do. Remember, this is not a resume, you are allowed to come up with "outside of the box" examples, such as perhaps you are skilled at being a good companion for your dog, or you are especially good at cheering up a friend when she is feeling upset, or you are excellent at doing a yoga pose. Of course, feel free to list your traditional resume-type skills as well.

Make a list of all of the key informational resources at your disposal

What type of information do you have access to? Perhaps you have access to the internet, libraries, books and magazines, encyclopedias, dictionaries, or experts. Writing this down will help to show yourself that you have many outlets available to help you acquire information and solve problems, even when you don't know how to do it immediately. Through the internet and the fact that most directories of information are searchable through typing in keywords, we live in a time when locating information is easier than it has ever been. If we don't know how to solve a problem through our own knowledge and experiences, we should not view this as an excuse to give up.

Open up communications with an expert

When you have a problem, and you have searched online and read books and still not been able to resolve it, seek out an expert who may be able to help. Often, people become frustrated quite quickly when they are unable to resolve a problem. Then they end up going to friends and relatives for advice. They mean well, but if they are not experts in the topic, then they are unlikely to know much more than you yourself would. Many experts will have an email address available online – briefly state your problem and what you have done to try to resolve it, then ask if they could help with this. This exercise will show you that you are able to extend the power of what you can do by reaching out to experts. Of course, if one expert does not respond or cannot help, you should be prepared to ask another.

For a problem you are dealing with right now, make a list of all that you can do to overcome it

What is a problem that you are dealing with right now? What information can you look up that would help to resolve it? What actions can you take? What options are immediately available to you? Who can help you to resolve this? Is there a record anywhere of similar problems that have occurred in the past? If so, how were they resolved? Is this a problem that requires immediate action, or do you have time to figure it out? If you need resources, how can you get them?

Ask what you can do, determine the best course of action, and then do it. Also, remember to think of your problems as *opportunities* – for learning, for improvement, and for testing your abilities.

THOUGHT #4

Focus on What You Have, *Not* on What You Do Not Have

"Do not spoil what you have by desiring what you have not; remember that what you now have was once among the things you only hoped for." – Epicurus

What You Can Do is Based on What You Have

In the prior section we focused on what you can do. However, what you can do is often limited by what you have access to. Therefore, it makes sense to pay close attention to what we have over what we do not have.

In the modern age, we are easily able to see all that we do *not* have. We can immediately go to the internet to see videos of people driving cars more expensive than the houses we live in, and we can find mansions that cost more than the money we could hope to earn in a hundred lifetimes.

We are constantly reminded of all of the things that we do not have, but this is not the right focus. When we focus on what we do not have, we end up becoming obsessed with wanting these things, because we know that other people have them. We become jealous and envious of them and this just brings out a dark energy from within us. This will either make us bitter, or propel us in the mindless pursuit of things, encouraging us to horde and to live selfishly.

Instead, we would be better served by remembering all of the things that we do have in our lives. What do you have in your life? What friends and family do you have? What knowledge, skills, and abilities do you have? Focusing on what you have will likely make you realize that you already have many of the most important things that you will ever need. Instead of seeking new things endlessly, you should be grateful for what you have in front of you right now.

When we reflect deeply, often we will become aware that the people and things present in our lives right now are worth more to us than all the rest of the world combined.

The Problem with Wanting More

Gautama Buddha taught that suffering (or *dukkha*) is universal and this is because of attachment to a desire. You are attached to wanting a specific outcome, or wanting a specific thing, so when you do not get it, you suffer. This is an example of focusing on the things you do not have, wanting those things, and craving them. If you can stop the craving, you can stop the suffering. It's as simple as this.

My point here is *not* that we cannot want, desire, or have goals. The point is that we have to wake up and understand that these desires are endless in their cycles. They are never fully satisfied, and never go away. When I was a child, I wanted a video game, then I wanted the next one, then I wanted the new video game system that just came out, then the next game and the next system. This is the same pattern we all go through even as adults, but often with more expensive items. For example, you may have noticed such a pattern with: clothing, shoes, TVs, computers, cars, houses, and so forth.

Perhaps we should be using our energy for a greater good, not for things that ultimately only benefit us personally, and only for fleeting moments. We should be cautious even of expenses that seem necessary, such as a house. If you upgrade from a 3-bedroom house to a 4-bedroomone, is this really making a big difference in your quality of life? Will you feel like this isn't good enough either and want a 5-bedroom house in a few years? Are you taking a big risk, buying a house that you can barely afford, risking your peace of mind and stability in the quest to gain just a little bit more?

There is something called *hedonic adaptation*, which has been researched by Shane Frederick and George Lowenstein. This term means that when you acquire a better life and more things, this becomes the new normal. You arrive at the same level of happiness or unhappiness, and the same level of satisfaction or dissatisfaction as you had been at in the past. Even upon making great progress, having more income and acquiring more things, you will feel like you still need a better life and more things. Then, when you acquire this better life and more things, this again becomes the new normal for you. The cycle repeats over and over, and you will always feel like you need more.

It will never be enough.

What breaks the cycle? Simply focusing on what you have already, appreciating that instead of always focusing on what you don't have that you would like to have.

What Do We All Have?

I would like for you to now consider the things that we all have and should be grateful for:

The Mind

Your mind is the most powerful tool you have. Regardless of which resources may come and go, your mind will always be there. You can use your mind to be rational, emotional, creative, logical, intuitive, and humorous, to name a few of the abilities that we all have.

Your mind is more powerful than any supercomputer. You have 100 billion neurons (or brain cells) in your brain which can form more than 100 trillion connections.

Life

Do not take this for granted, as none of us have an unlimited life or unlimited time. The life we have now is a gift (See Thought #7), and our task is to make the most of it.

Possessions

Of course, when most of us think of what we have, we think of our possessions, but I would argue that these are some of the most unimportant things that we have. For the possessions that you have, you may find that a few core items are of huge importance for you, but that most of them are not highly important. My most important items are simply my phone and my computer. I spend a lot of my time on these every day. And most of the rest of the items that I use on a daily basis are for simple needs – toothbrush, clothing, dishes, food, bed, etc. Ask yourself: *What do I have, what do I use most, and what am I grateful for?*

Loved ones

Our loved ones are the people who we often count on the most. Whenever we have great troubles, they are there to help us. This also works the other way around – if they have issues, we are ready to help them.

The loved ones in our lives will not be there forever, and so it is important to remember them and spend some time with them, or at least to keep communications open with them. *Who are the people in your life who you love most?*

Values

Values are mentioned here because they are a key part of who we are, and sometimes we need a reminder of what it is that we value. They are important because they help to provide us with a sort of compass, to guide us along the right path when we are not sure what to do. For many tough decisions in life, they can be made simple by asking: *Which choice stays true to my values?*

Some values that you may have are: honesty, persistence, respect, kindness, balance, fairness, friendship, family, optimism, peace, and faith. You must always remember to have your values with you and to do your best to live up to them. *What values do you have?*

Borrowing What We Have

Even for the things we do have, understand that we are just borrowing them. When you have something, whatever it is, its days are numbered. Therefore, we must learn to appreciate the things that we have now, instead of worrying about all the things that we wish to have. Ultimately, everything that we have is temporary and will perish – being aware of this fact can bring peace and understanding that no matter how much you acquire, it will all be gone one day. At first this realization can be distressing, but on deeper reflection we can see that this just means we must enjoy everything that we have while we still can.

To help drive the point home, consider how long some typical items will last you:

Food – from a few days in the refrigerator to a few years if canned

Computer – 5-10 years

Cash – 5-15 years, until the bills wear down – of course, more money is printed to replace it

Sofa – 7-15 years

Washer and dryer – 10-15 years

Car – 10-15 years

Books – 40-100+ years

Human life – 50-100 years

House – 50-100+ years

Land – indefinitely

Dreaming of What Could Have Been

We often think, or we may hear people say, "If only I had had another child, I would be happier." "If only I had taken the other job offer instead, I would be happier." "If only I had gone to a more prestigious university, I would be happier." We become obsessed with what we could have had, and we can't enjoy what we do have because of it. If you stop and see these mental patterns, you will see that we are causing our own miseries in this way.

What we fail to see is that if you change one thing, you change everything. We have no way of knowing what the results would have been if we had done one thing differently in our lives. You may *not* have met your spouse, had your kids, learned a valuable life lesson, etc. Everything could have changed from then on, for the better or for the worse. Thus, we should be grateful and not dream about the way things could have been, because in the end, even if we had made what we think would have been a better decision, the outcome could have been worse on that other path.

Keep in mind that events which seem good do not always have good outcomes. And events that seem bad do not always have bad outcomes. Thus, we should not feel too strongly that we always know the best way. No matter how we live our lives, there is always room for surprise in the final outcomes. We must always remember that we do not have all the knowledge or all the answers.

Instead of dreaming of what could have been, or regretting what happened, we must learn to accept the reality of what we have in front of us. When we allow our minds to obsess over different time periods, then we fail to do the best that we can *with what we have* right now.

Remember this: Wanting things to be different than what they are is one of our greatest sources of misery.

The Secret to Happiness

The secret to happiness is in redefining it. We need to learn to stop wanting all of the things that are ultimately not so important, and instead to have gratitude for the important things that we already have – perhaps love, a home, good friends, food in the fridge, and a job that pays well enough. Our task is to learn to want what we already have.

The person who stops you and explains how he will never be happy unless he fulfills all of his dreams, and proceeds to discuss numerous fantastical and vivid dreams and how they all must happen exactly as this person wishes, is destined to never be happy. Whereas the person who tells you that he is going to do everything in his power to accomplish his dream, but in the end if he doesn't accomplish what he had hoped, he will still be happy, is a person who should be happy no matter what happens.

We make the choice to be happy or not. Our inner dialogue makes the difference. Pay attention to any phrases you tell yourself that go something like, "I will never be happy unless…" Your thinking of it makes it true. Instead, choose to think thoughts such as, "I choose to be happy because I have…" In fact, any time you are feeling unhappy, I would challenge you to get a notebook and to start writing that phrase: "I choose to be happy because I have…" and to keep writing down the reasons that you choose to be happy *until you feel happy*.

Do not think this is a silly exercise. Writing is a powerful tool. Our thoughts sometimes go every which direction without any real structure. But when you put thoughts to paper, writing makes them real.

The biggest mistake we make is that we chase happiness. And when we do this, happiness grows legs and it runs away from us. We want a certain title, or a certain blissful and carefree feeling, or a romantic partner that does everything the way we prefer, or to own a large house, or to have a certain number in our bank account. We want this and so we chase it, but we are never quite fulfilled, never quite happy. Always chasing more, and more, and more. This is because we get stuck on the idea that we needed something to feel fulfilled and happy. But perhaps we never needed much other than what we already had. Perhaps what we already had was more than enough.

Remember this: We can choose to be happy with what we have, or to be unhappy with what we chase.

Be Grateful for What You Have

Practice your gratitude

There are many, many things to be grateful for. Be grateful for your health, for the life you get to experience, and for the things that you have. Be grateful for family members and friends, for not living in the middle of a natural disaster right now, and for having the money to buy the important things you need. Be grateful for clean water and for vaccinations that immunize us from diseases that would have easily killed us. If you have failed at something miserably – be grateful for the chance to try again and that no one has died for your mistakes. Even if someone has died for your mistakes, be grateful for the opportunity to teach others about the grave consequences of making that mistake, to prevent future suffering. Be grateful.

If you happen to be in prison being punished for having ended a life or for any crime, then be grateful for the opportunity to reflect and to grow as a person. Even if you are being sentenced to death for a crime you did *not* commit – be grateful. Be grateful for the life you were able to experience, instead of bitter about the life that will be unrightfully cut short.

What other option do we have than to be grateful – does being hateful improve our lives? Does being bitter improve it? On the contrary, it wastes the precious life we have. Be grateful, no matter what.

We don't know what we have until it's gone

Think about something or someone that you have taken for granted – it could be a family member, your health, friends, a nice home, that you have a comfortable amount of savings in the bank, clothing, or food.

Consider that food is easily accessible to much of society at this point. But even there, it comes at a cost that goes beyond money. It comes at the cost of the life of animals. The Native Americans were known to use every single portion of the animal, eating all of the edible parts and using the inedible parts such as bones for another function – combs, cutlery, jewelry, musical instruments, etc. They did not take their meals for granted, and so they were grateful for each one.

Now, that same territory where the Native Americans lived is one where the most food waste takes place. Food is no longer something we are grateful just to have, as the Native Americans would have been. Since food is almost guaranteed, we now treat it as if it were something that we deserved, that we feel entitled to. We fail to stop and think that we should still be grateful. Any number of issues could happen which would make it difficult for us to get food – financial issues, new diseases that contaminate crops, or imbalances in the ecosystem causing major species to go extinct. In general, people may not become grateful again until there is a problem with getting this food.

What is something you have you taken for granted? How will you practice gratitude from here on?

What Other People Have is a Distraction

A woman in her early 20s called into Gary Vaynerchuk's show, #AskGaryVee. The young woman who called in explained that she was graduating from college and that she had great ambitions to start a business and to be highly successful, but she had a sort of mental barrier, blocking her from actually getting started in pursuing this dream. She then explained that she was worried because she was aware that some people had attained great success at a very young age, and she felt insecure about her abilities because of it.

Gary responded with some of his best advice:

"Every second you spend thinking about what somebody else has is taking away from time that you could create something for yourself."

When you think of it this way, you will see just how wasteful it is to worry about what someone else has and what someone else is achieving. The bottom line here is to *not* focus on what others have. Focus on what you have. Focus on where you want to be. Focus on what you can do to get there, with what you have. If you don't have something right now, make a plan to get it.

As another point, we all know that people keep up appearances in public, but you have no way of knowing what happens behind closed doors. Couples that appear perfect in public could have intense arguments every day back at home. People who seem calm and collected and to have it all, could be quietly insecure and paranoid that they will lose everything soon, secretly feeling that they are not as good as other people think they are. Don't waste time, life, and energy thinking about what other people have. Or better yet, don't waste it thinking about what other people *appear* to have. They may seem to have perfect lives, but that perfection often falls to pieces under scrutiny.

Remember this: Stop wasting time on what you think others have, on the greatness that you think they are achieving. Focus on yourself. Focus on what you are going to achieve.

Control Your Desire to Have What Others Have...

Control your desires to have what others have, for these desires will lead to envy, which is a dark emotion. Instead of having a deep desire for what someone else has, replace this feeling with sharing joy for others – empathize with their joy. Learn to feel it as if it were your own. This is the difference between making friends and making enemies.

I have an older brother who is only 15 months older. I can recall at a young age sometimes wanting something that he had. Perhaps I would want a toy he had, or if he accomplished something, I might also feel jealous. That feeling may have been more for the positive attention he would receive than for whatever it was that he had acquired or accomplished.

I also remember from a young age realizing that these were dark emotions, to want what my brother had. Because the thoughts tend to get darker from there on. Perhaps you know someone who has spoken like this with you: "Why does she deserve it? I've done more work for it than she ever did. She is not even that good. I could do better if they gave me a chance." With such thoughts, it's not much of a stretch before the envious person feels justified in sabotaging the person she is envious of. Even if it is a teammate, or a friend, or a sibling, she starts to view this person as a competitor or perhaps even an enemy. Of course, my thoughts were not so dark as a child, but I did know that I did not want to have any bad thoughts about my brother. I did not want to start down that dark road.

Even at a young age, I decided that I should be genuinely happy for his accomplishments, as I would wish him to be genuinely happy for mine. And it has worked. I have never felt that he was envious of something I have done, and I have always felt that we could both be happy and proud for each other's accomplishments. We should seek this sharing in each other's joy with most of our life relationships. This is much better than feeling jealous, resentful, and sending negative thoughts to someone else.

My warning here is that the dark thoughts can spread more quickly than you might imagine. I have seen people attain amazing successes, and rather than others congratulating this person, people would focus on why the success was easy because this person was privileged, or that the success was undeserved, or even that the success only occurred because of unethical or perhaps illegal activities. In most cases where I have heard such comments, it was evident to me that the comments were based more in jealousy than in facts. We must learn to feel that someone else's success is my success. Someone else's joy is my joy. Learn to feel proud for being the brother, sister, client, employee, neighbor, or friend of someone who has made a great accomplishment. Someone else doing well does not mean that you are doing poorly. Someone else being greater, does not mean that you are lesser.

This is a daily practice. To undo thinking habits, you must catch yourself in the act of thinking the *bad thoughts*. When you are thinking "I'm sure he didn't deserve that raise. I should have gotten it," you must catch yourself, and realize that this is a dark path you do not want to go on. Instead, congratulate this person from your heart and wish him well. Perhaps even ask for advice to increase your chances of getting a raise. In the end, you may discover that this person *did* deserve it more than you did.

This is one of the most important life skills I ever learned. I have seen many people fall into its traps, creating misery for themselves and others without much reason. Learn to stop these dark thoughts early on, or they may overcome you.

Many of us will understand the points made above, but we will enter a competition or play in a game against someone and become angry and upset when we lose. We will feel that we deserved the win, not them. Of course, this is not the right path.

Even if someone beats you at a game or competition or anything, do not take it personally. Do not be hurt by this. Do not feel inferior. Learn to acquire knowledge from those who best you. Ask the winner for advice on how you can improve. Figure out why you lost, and why your competitor won. Congratulate him and absorb all that he knows so that you can become his equal or better, and then repeat this process over and over with each time that you lose to someone. To become the best, you must become comfortable with not always being the best. Do not become bitter, jealous, wishing harm on the one who beat you, and being a sore loser when you are outperformed. Learn to look forward to the challenge and to the journey of becoming better than your current self. It wasn't meant to be easy, or we would all be the best.

Remember this: When you lose, don't get bitter, get better. Then come back and win.

The Unknowing Teacher

The *Unknowing Teacher* is something that many of us have in our lives and fail to be grateful for. This is someone who teaches you but without meaning to. Usually, this person isn't a teacher by profession, and they are not teaching you specific lessons on purpose. Instead, they teach you based on the poor decisions that they have made in their lives, and you are the one who gets to see the results of those choices.

When we see people who have made poor choices in their lives, we can see why they now have a bad situation in life. They retired too young and now they are broke; they didn't pay attention to their children and now those children have grown to become criminals; they took everything personally and now they are perpetually unhappy; they drank every weekend instead of pursuing their dreams, and now their life is filled with regret.

The unknowing teacher is someone who teaches us a lot about what we should *not do*, how we should *not live*, and *what to avoid* in our lives. Such a person is a great resource to have and to witness, because sometimes we need a reminder of where the bad paths in life will lead us. Be grateful for these people when you see them and learn from their example.

If someone very close to you is an unknowing teacher – perhaps a parent or a sibling, do not feel sorry for yourself. Simply through your everyday exposure to such a person, you will be able to immunize yourself from having to lead the same type of life. You will see all the bad behaviors that lead to the negative outcomes and learn that this is not the life for you.

Remember this: Heed the lessons of the unknowing teacher carefully, or risk becoming one yourself.

Exercises

What loved ones are you most grateful for?

Make a list of the top 5-10 most important people in your life and ask yourself if you have been giving them the proper attention that they deserve. Do these people know how important they are to you? When they need help, do you offer it? Are you generally available for their needs, or are you always too busy with something else?

What values do you have which are most important for you to live by?

Write out a list of your top 5-15 values that are most important for you to live by. Remember that if they are your values, they are a part of who you are. It is critical that you live by them, or otherwise you are living against your own beliefs. To live a happy, fulfilling life, our thoughts, beliefs, words, and actions should all line up.

Here are some examples of values to consider: dependability, passion, loyalty, commitment, motivation, good humor, open-mindedness, honesty, creativity, positivity, respect, fitness, courage, education, perseverance, service, environmentalism, authenticity, fairness, happiness, community, kindness, love, loyalty, peace, spirituality, wisdom, security.

Make an inventory of everything that you have

The task of writing down everything you own may be overwhelming if you have acquired many items through the years. If it's too much, start with a single room in your home. Make an inventory of absolutely everything that you have in one room. This exercise may show you that you already have too many things right now. Or you may realize that the things that you thought would fulfill a need, ended up never being used. Often, we acquire what we have without being fully conscious of why we have it. Sometimes we acquire more and more, without having a good reason for it.

Make a list of the things you use on a regular basis, out of the items that you have

After you have listed out the items that you own, make a list of the ones that you use regularly. You will probably find that you are using no more than 20% of your items, perhaps even less. This exercise will show us that many of the items we acquire have no real purpose. Their purpose becomes to fill up space, or to be a distraction and waste your time. We should aim to become conscious of what it is that we have and why we have it, and to remove those things that are solely taking up space.

Make a list of all the things you are grateful to have

Think about what some things are that you are grateful to have. If you struggle, run through your typical day in your mind and pay attention to the small things that you tend to take for granted. Doing this exercise will help to remind you to be grateful for the things you have. It is important that we always appreciate what we have while we still have it. While making your list, keep in mind things we often take for granted such as access to hot water, a bed to sleep in, and clean air to breathe.

THOUGHT #5

Focus on the Present, *Not* on the Past and Future

"Do not dwell in the past, do not dream of the future, concentrate the mind on the present moment." – Buddha

The Present Moment is All We Have

The prior Thought was to focus on what you have, and we must realize that all we really have is the present moment. The past has already happened, and it remains with us through our memories and our interpretations of events. The future has yet to happen, and so we do not have it yet. As much as we don't like to think of it, a sudden tragedy can rob us of the future, even if we are young and healthy. As a reminder, I do not view this news pessimistically – instead I see it as a positive, so that we can always remember to make the most of every moment, to live our lives to the fullest.

Before continuing, I would like you to ponder the following questions, and to answer "Yes" to the one that most accurately represents you:

Do you like having done what you did?

Do you like doing what you're doing, while you are doing it?

Do you like fantasizing about doing something?

The first statement keeps your focus in the past, the second one keeps it on the present, and the third one keeps it on the future. *Where is your mind typically focused?*

The Nature of Goals

Goals are so common in modern life that we tend to assume that they are an essential part of success. But are they really as useful as we think? I have goals, as I am sure essentially everyone does. Nonetheless, I feel that there is too much focus on goals, and not enough focus on the process of what we are doing. Isn't it more important to do our best in the moment, rather than always focusing on goals, which are just the consequences of our thoughts and actions?

The main issue with goals is that by definition it is a focus on a desired end state. You may be able to influence an end state, but of course you do not have full control over it. Strangely enough, for most people this means they will be in a state of unhappiness and tension while they have not met their goal. They will need to meet this goal to feel relieved and happy. But this happiness does not last, because as humans, we always need something to work toward. We understand deep down that the work, or the true objective, is never complete. Even after the death of an important person working on an important goal, the goal will probably still be incomplete, and other people will need to continue making progress on that objective.

In a typical person's life, if you lose five pounds you may be happy, but you understand that this is not a permanent accomplishment. Meeting the goal puts you in the uncomfortable position of fulfilling something, yet being aware that at any moment you could fail and regain the weight. If you had instead focused on a process of being happy with eating healthier foods and with an exercise routine that you enjoyed, then you would not have needed to worry much about meeting a goal. In focusing on the moment and the process, you would be more likely to actually meet your goal of losing the weight.

If you get a raise at work, again, this is not necessarily a permanent accomplishment. You could get fired or demoted at any point in the future. If you finish reading an introductory book about physics, you feel good, but at the same time you realize that you know very little about many in depth topics in physics, and so there is still much more to learn. If you get a PhD in sociology, you may feel great, but there is still much more work to do – you may pursue a postdoctoral degree or apply for a teaching position. Either path still presents many obstacles to you, as the PhD was never the endpoint that it seemed to be.

Meeting a goal, even a big goal, is often not as satisfying as we would wish. We have the same problem as with acquiring material items. The more goals we meet, the more goals we feel we need to meet, and we chase a sense of happiness that is always running away from us, rather than attaining a true happiness. As a friend once mentioned to me, checking things off of a To-Do list can feel highly rewarding. I can agree that it provides a sense of accomplishment, but is it really an accomplishment to check off items? We always have stuff to do, but the real question is if this is getting us anywhere. If meeting all of your goals and To-Dos keeps you in a static state of unfulfillment, or in a sense of fulfillment but without having accomplished much, then the goals are not helping. Or if you feel as if you are unable to keep up with all of your To-Dos, then you will feel even worse, and the goals instead become a constant reminder of your failures.

The trick then is to focus on the enjoyment of a process. Make the "goal" to do your best in every moment of every day, on the tasks and objectives that are most important to you. To continue with the example above, if you would like to lose weight, you may commit to jogging for a half a mile a day at first. Commit to the process and enjoy this as you go, rather than holding on to the need to lose a certain number of pounds. Run routes where you can enjoy the scenery. Run with a partner who can help to make it more fun. If you are too used to goal-thinking, your goal becomes to enjoy the process of working out and eating healthy.

If you don't believe that goals are *not* the solution to living the good life, then listen to someone who has met likely two of the most common goals that people will have: to be rich and famous. Here is what Jim Carrey, the famous actor, has said:

"I think everybody should get rich and famous and do everything they ever dreamed of so they can see that it's not the answer."

Apparently, meeting these two grand goals, and even other goals of doing what you dreamed of, are not nearly as fulfilling as people would think. I am sure that it creates many problems too, perhaps unwanted attention, unwanted requests for money, and the media stating untrue and harmful things about your life. Also, it will be difficult to know if people like you only for your celebrity and money, or if they like you for who you actually are.

Here is something to consider. Once you have met all of your goals, what becomes your goal then? The sad reality is that all you have to do is follow celebrity news to find out – many turn to drugs, as this may be the only thing that can help them to hit a greater high than what they have already accomplished. You can see that we are naturally unsatisfied even when we have made our dreams come true. And of course, we are unsatisfied while our dreams have not come true as well. The true goal then is to learn to be happy with what we have, and with all that we are given in the present moment.

You may feel conflicted, still thinking that goals must be good. This is because in society, almost everyone pursues goals, and obviously some good does come out of this. But think of a goal that you have right now. Perhaps you would like to get your diploma or to become a manager at your job. You are sure that everything will fall into place when you arrive at that level. People tend to think that they will be fulfilled and happy, and they usually are, but just for a short while. When you meet such goals, you may even feel elated, but it doesn't last. It's like expecting a new relationship to make you happy. It probably will for a few weeks or months, but then comes the real work, which is when many people will wonder if continuing with the relationship is even worth it.

We want the happiness without the work, but instead we must find things in our life where we *want* to work at it. Find the relationships where you are happy when you work to brighten the day of your partner. Find the job and the life path where you want to work at it and you look forward to the challenges. If you are chasing outcomes, it either isn't the right path, or you are making things harder on yourself than they need to be.

The real challenge of life is learning to appreciate the moment. Meeting goals only gives us a fleeting sense of happiness, which we always have to chase with more and more goals. True happiness, however, is not something we should chase. The more we chase it, the more it runs away from us. Happiness is in the moments, and often the little ones that we tend to take for granted. We have to learn to take those little moments and give them the due attention and love that they truly deserve.

Remember this: Happiness is in the here and now – there is nothing to chase.

Why Should We *Not* Focus Too Much on the Past?

The past is great, right? We all have at least some memories that we are fond of. I'm sure we can all enjoy reflecting on the past occasionally. But the main issue is if we allow our thinking of the past to interfere with what we are doing now. If you are too nostalgic, longing for the past, then you will not be able to make the best of the present moment.

When I was accepted to Purdue University to pursue my undergraduate degree many years ago, I began as a biology major (later I switched to psychology). In my freshman year, I met several students who enjoyed talking about how smart they had been at their high school. They were at the top of the class, with perfect GPAs. These were bright people, but I got the sense that we had reached a point where everyone was smart. These students were holding onto the idea of needing to be the best, and they fantasized about how they had had that in their high school. They seemed to be avoiding the reality that this was a different level in college, with much greater challenges. Many students were used to being the best, but we could not *all* be the best anymore. In this setting, most of us would become merely average. By focusing on the present moment and forgetting about the past, we would be able to perform at our personal best. However, if we clung to our past and how we were the top of the top in our high schools, we would feel inferior and struggle to keep up with what was required of us here in the now.

This daydreaming of how things were better in the past is common when we are thrust into a new and difficult environment. But what about the opposite scenario? What if instead, something greatly troubling happened in our past, and we find it difficult to get away from this? We may constantly replay this event in our minds, adding to our own suffering. We may also wish that we could change what happened, beating ourselves up over it. Obviously, this is destructive and counterproductive. When this happens, what can we do to regain control of our minds and to have a positive outlook?

Here, the dilemma is similar as with the classic psychological conundrum where someone tells you *not* to think of a pink elephant. The outcome of course is that you can think of nothing but the pink elephant. Similarly, a person who has lived through a trauma may tell himself that he doesn't want to think about what happened, and paradoxically he can never get away from it. He may think about it nonstop by the very fact that he focuses on *not* wanting to think about it. I cannot speak as to how to recover from deeply traumatic events, but a key way to stop thinking about troubling memories in general is to learn to live fully in the present. When your mind is filled with being in the present, it is difficult for it to process the past at the same time. When old memories rise up, you can meditatively bring yourself back to the present moment. This of course will take some training, to learn to override your old habits and patterns. The shift here is in the mindset – you are not avoiding a disturbing memory, instead you are filling your mind with all that is right here, right now.

Learn to tell yourself: The past is in the past. I cannot change it. Instead of worrying about it, I should live in the here and now. I can control my life *now*. I can change what I want to change *now*. I can do my best *now*. The past is most useful in the lessons that I can learn from what happened. But it stops being useful if thinking about it prevents me from living my life to the fullest in the *present moment*.

Tell yourself this until you fully understand and embody the message, and you have allowed the past and its pains to melt away.

People who look too much to the past, and agonize over every mistake they have made, and think about what they could've-should've-would've done, tend to be depressed. If you are depressed, then you are clearly not living life to the fullest. And your task is to stop the cycle of miserable thoughts, and to learn to live in the present, and experience the joys that come with it.

The power of living in the Now is the power to *not* need to be defined by your past mistakes, to *not* need to be defined by your past actions or inactions. You do *not* need to be who you were yesterday, or the day before that if that is not working for you. You can change everything just by deciding that you will not create the same outcomes that you were creating in the past. You and you alone have the power to change your thoughts and actions to make something new. You should not be afraid of trying something new because even if this fails you, you will find the right path eventually. Doing the same old thing that didn't work before is just creating more agony, and this is a pattern that needs to stop. It stops Now. It stops in the Here and Now, and nowhere else.

Why Should We *Not* Focus Too Much on the Future?

I will admit that I used to have a problem with focusing excessively on the past at times, and on the future at times. I would find myself depressed the times that I could not get over the past, and anxious the times that I could not stop worrying about the future. There is no magic pill to stop your mind from doing this and to turn your focus to the present. But as is often said, the first step to overcoming a problem is to realize that it exists. If you practice noticing that your mind is away from the present moment, and on guiding it back to now, you will get better and better at living in the present moment. But this must be a daily practice.

When we are always looking toward the future, similarly as with the past, this means we are not living fully in the now, which again, the now is all that we have.

Ask yourself this: *If I am not right here, Right Now, then where am I?* This simple question can help you to realize that there is nowhere else you need to be.

Understand that people who focus too much on the future tend to feel a need for control. They want to control what is going to happen in the future, so they live in states of anxiety, of tension, of wanting things to be in a certain way, and they are disappointed when they do not turn out that way. This leads to a perpetual unhappiness. Thought #1 is to focus on what you can control, *not* on what you cannot control, and of course we cannot control the future. We do not have that much power. We also do not have control over the outcomes of our actions. And so we must learn to let go of our need for this control, and just let it be.

Even when it seems positive, thinking of the future is essentially a wishing of things to be a certain way. When I was a child, perhaps 8 or 9 years old, my father would sometimes tell me: "You will go to college one day and you will have a great career in whatever field you choose." This is a very positive message, but strangely enough, the focus of putting things into the far future gave me a sense of pressure, even at 8 or 9 years old. I can recall sometimes feeling anxious, wondering if I could possibly sit down and study for hours on very difficult topics, and wondering if I would be smart enough to handle it. I was too young to realize that by the point I was old enough to go to college, I would be ready – there was no need to worry about the future.

The most important point for you to understand is that you should do your best in the moment on the tasks in front of you. If you do, things will tend to fall into place. In contrast, a mind stuck in the past or worried about the future will fail to make the best of present opportunities.

We tend to live in a very future-oriented society, making plans for what we are doing in the upcoming hours, making plans for tomorrow, for the coming weeks, sometimes for the coming months or even years. All of this is in the future, right? Does that make it wrong to think about the future and to plan? Should our minds *always* be in the present? No, of course you do not need to always be in the present, but we need to do it more. Having plans for your future is the disciplined and responsible thing to do. But you have to understand that if your mind is always in the future, then when are you actually present? When are your mind and body both at the same place at the same time? Even when you make plans, find a way to be present with it. If you need an hour a week to plan your upcoming week, then do that and be fully present while you do it. But don't allow wondering about future plans to hijack too much of your day. Aim to live more of your life in the now, for this is all we really have.

How can we live more in the present, and less in the past and future, when this has become a bad habit?

In my life, my mind naturally wanders, and I drift to the past and future, but I do not agonize over either. If you find yourself agonizing, you have to stop and question, *What am I doing to myself? Why am I doing this to myself? I am in control, and I can stop this needless agonizing with my own thoughts.* There is no need to punish yourself further for what your mind does naturally, but when this happens, just relax, take a breath, and shift your mind to the present. This is the meditative way. Through meditation we do not punish ourselves for our aimless thoughts, our irrelevant thoughts, or even our negative thoughts. We gently bring the mind back to the present and continue with our lives as peacefully and joyously as we can.

Remember this: Allow yourself more time to be in the Now, to enjoy the Now, and to not always need to be in your head, in the past, in the future, thinking of what was, what could be, what may be, what should be. Allow yourself more Now Time, to relish in all that is happening Right Now.

The Fragmented Mind

The fragmented mind is the mind that is overworked, over-worried, jumping from task to task in a frenzy. It involves thinking such as:

I can't forget about what they told me to do, but wait, I have to do this first. No, but that needed to get done too because if not everything else will fall to pieces. But if I don't do this other thing, everyone will hate me. It's getting late. I have to go. Oh no, the car is out of gas. I better get gas first. Wait, there is no time for that. I'm already late for a meeting where I was supposed to speak!

The fragmented mind tries to be everywhere at once and accomplishes nothing in the end. It is a disease of the times, with so much going on that our minds are overworked and over-distracted, yet of course failing. We simply have to take a breath, and stop and realize that if we are everywhere, trying to be everything to everyone, then we are accomplishing nothing, and the mind is truly nowhere. The mind becomes absent from the present. Rather, we must *become present in the moment* for our minds to be able to work properly.

When you are at dinner and a family member tells you about his or her day, and your mind wanders to problems with work, with neighbors, with family, or to problems with your ability to cope with your problems, then *Where is your mind, really? What are you really accomplishing?* I mention this to help us wake up, to help us get back to that present moment which so often escapes us. When you are dying, the present moment is precious, but to the rest of us we tend to treat the present as if it had very little value. We need to remember its value, that it is all we have.

Do Your Best in Every Moment of Every Day

Learn from the past but do not dwell on it. Plan for the future but do not obsess over it. Live more of your life in the present, as it is the only place that life can be lived. The only thing that exists is the Here and Now.

The power of the human memory can cause you to endlessly relive and be crippled by your past. Let it go and learn to forgive and possibly forget your past mistakes. This is easier said than done. It needs to become a willful and conscious process, and eventually it will become an automatic habit.

There is a powerful need in humans to escape our lives which can make us focus too much on the future, thinking that this is where all of our problems will be solved, and that we will be eternally happy. We must see this for what it is, a mirage that distracts us from what truly matters, and instead turn our focus to the present moment. This is where life happens.

Tell yourself this when you are losing presence: *What I am doing right now is worth all of my attention, energy, and commitment. If it is not, I must stop doing it and do that thing which is indeed worth all of my attention, energy, and commitment.*

Even if you are truly unhappy with the present and you find yourself wanting to escape it, you must understand that escaping it will not make it better.

In times when you feel like everything has gone wrong and you want to escape, think to yourself: *At this moment on this day, I choose to transform my life and turn it all around. I do not need to continue with the same old patterns, I can change and be who I choose to be. I can build myself into who I want to be. If I have been destroyed, I can be reborn and start from the beginning, as all great empires were begun with a single brick.*

The alternative to focusing on the present is to focus on outcomes. However, any outcomes that we hyper-focus on will become elusive. Happiness is often viewed as an outcome. But I think we can learn to generate our own inner joy that does not require external events. Money is an outcome for many. However, for me it is tied directly to my ability to be in the present and to do my best in every moment. Success is generally viewed as an outcome, although again this is based on my ability to have presence of mind, and to do the best that I can in the present moment. These all appear to be outcomes but are actually based on our ability to be fully present. Is it possible that the secret to happiness, success, wealth, and possibly health and other positive attributes, is in being fully present? Try it, and you tell me.

Overcome the Mind

> "Never confuse movement with progress. Because you can run in place and not get anywhere."
> – Denzel Washington

The real question is how to actually become present. Understand that the mind is the enemy of presence. The mind is like a time-traveling machine that will take you everywhere but here. It has magical properties and can do almost anything. Unfortunately, we rarely know how to tap into its powers effectively. The mind is like a tiny car with an astronomical amount of horsepower – it is capable of staying still, but it struggles with this because there is a great temptation to use its full power in a reckless fashion.

The mind at its full power can generate an immense amount of energy and activity, but the issue is that much of this can be counterproductive. Your mind may naturally take you in too many directions, fragmenting itself. It may take you deep into insecurities and failures of your past. It may create wonderful future possibilities that you fall in love with and become distracted with. The mind may feel that it deserves and is owed something, and become upset when it is not given this, causing a wild storm of emotions. All of these result in a lack of progress.

The key way your mind makes progress is when it forgets about all of its amazing powers and instead elects to remain still. It elects to see the present moment with crystal clarity, and to perform the necessary actions to make progress. For the mind to progress and overcome itself, it must do that which it wants to do least and needs to do most (See 6th Thought): it must be calm, still, and present.

As you have seen, becoming still and present is one way to overcome the mind. Another key way to overcome the mind is to realize that your thoughts are not you. When you have a thought, that thought is just a manifestation of you, as if you were to take a sheet of paper and write something down. The writing on the paper is not you, it is a manifestation of you, as are your thoughts. A key to overcoming the powers of your mind is to understand that you are not your thoughts. You can choose some of your thoughts, but sometimes you do not choose them, and they are just there. Learn to be present and to observe your thinking, without assuming that your thinking is you.

Remember this: Use your mind's immense powers and capabilities carefully, or your mind will use you.

How to Be Present

We all know how to be present. We did this as young children, but we grew out of that phase as we learned the full power of what our minds were capable of. Unfortunately, in losing presence, many of us became disordered rather than enlightened.

It feels silly to show you how to do something that you already know how to do, but let's proceed, to help you relearn that which was lost and forgotten.

To be present, observe nature. See the bird, and actually see the bird, not all that it is not. See the tree, and actually see the tree, not all that it is not. See the wind, and actually see the wind, not all that it is not. See the rose, and actually see the rose, not all that it is not. Train your sight in this way, to see what is, and not all that is not.

To be present, observe the spirit of things, not the spirit of all that is not. This time, see the bird, and see its spirit. See the tree, and see its spirit, see the rose, and see its spirit. Spirit is its true essence, not simply its physical properties. When we see people, we see the physical form, and a deeper spirit form – personality, emotion, and a being that is important just through the fact of being. However, we often fail to see this with nature. Train yourself to see it by observing carefully. The spirit is there in all living forms.

Note that I have guided you the reader to what to do, and what *not* to do, in efforts to make this as clear as day.

Do not just focus on sight. Repeat the above observations with the bird, the tree, the wind, the rose, and anything else, but this time focus intently on sounds, and then smells, and even touch if that is appropriate. Just as we see three-dimensionally, understand that with each sense we perceive, we add a dimension to life. This means that we are perceiving at least through the five dimensions of our traditional senses – sight, smell, hearing, touch, and taste. To begin, focus on one sense at a time. As you build in your powers of being present, you may eventually be able to perceive them fully all at once.

Let's go deeper into what it means to be fully present.

To be present will mean that you must learn to be absent of thought, and just be. The mind takes you to the past, the future, and everywhere but here. However, in order to be fully present, we must suspend thought. This takes intention, time, and training to master. When thoughts do come, allow them to pass *through* you rather than hanging onto them. Suspend all your worries, fears, hopes, dreams, goals, and concerns. Many of us feel that we need entertainment (such as a movie) to suspend this, but actually you can do it right now. Using entertainment only replaces our own thoughts and preoccupations with thoughts about something else.

One way to suspend thought is to focus internally on your breath, or on the sensations of your body – is there any tension? How does your hand feel? How does your leg feel? How does your foot feel? Focus on parts that you normally ignore – how do your eyes feel? How does your tongue feel? How do your fingernails feel? How do your ears feel? How does your heart feel? Focus on this to raise awareness of being, and to suspend thought.

The other way to suspend thought is to focus externally and intently on what is happening. It is ideal to focus on nature because there is so much vibrant life, so much happening if you truly stop and take notice. The clouds in the background that seem static are actually in motion if you pay attention. The blades of grass that seem irrelevant actually harbor smaller lifeforms, are food for life, provide cushioning for our shoes, and flow with the breeze. The animals that seem to be on a simpleminded quest for food are not always in its pursuit – sometimes they are just being, or they are at play. At night, each star twinkles in its own unique way. You don't need to go into the wilderness to experience nature. Step outside and observe your surroundings, go for a walk, or go to a park.

When you observe, notice how everything in nature is in the present moment. For nature, to lose presence means death. In Paris (where I am living as I write this), there are a great abundance of pigeons in the city. The pigeons here are comfortable with humans, walking on the ground near us, and the vast majority of humans are not a threat to these birds. Of course, the birds must be careful because we are so much bigger that it would be easy for us to harm them unintentionally.

The other day I was walking and I saw something unfortunate. A boy suddenly lunged forward, attempting to kick a pigeon, and the bird was just narrowly able to escape. That pigeon needed to be fully present to escape the attack. If it had become too comfortable or distracted somehow, it would have been horribly injured. Luckily, it maintained presence.

Be as present as you can be. Nature is fully present, and it teaches us every day if we are willing to learn from it.

Young children – perhaps younger than the child mentioned above, who was probably 8 years old – are also good examples of being present. I recently saw a 3-year-old child who had somehow become separated from his mother in a park. He was fully present, playing with a bush and the small bright red berries that it was filled with. He was so absorbed with the present moment of being with the bush, that he had no idea his mother had gone far enough ahead to be completely out of his sight. It was a wonderful sight to observe this child, as he had become one with nature. Do not worry: of course, his mother soon returned to him.

You may think that you don't have the time to be present. If that is the case, then I would challenge you to spend one minute per day on being fully present. When you have mastered this, try five minutes, then ten minutes, gradually moving up and up. You can practice this at any moment. It will be easier to do this when you are not at work, or not doing an important task, and not in a rush to get somewhere. Make some time every day to just be, and not need to perform a specific function.

Learn to Love the Present

Love is about acceptance. When you have your own child, you love that child whether he is good or bad. You accept the child for who he is now. You understand that he cannot be something other than who he is, right now. In time, he will grow and evolve and change, but right now, he is who he is.

The analogy here is the same for the present moment. We must learn to love the present, which means to accept the presence as it is. If you are in a place in your life that you are not happy with or not satisfied with, you must still accept that present as your reality. There is no way to change your present moment, it just is. Just as there is no way to change your child for another one, even if he has misbehaved. Remember that the present is here and cannot be un-here. You can't argue with the present. The present is here, and it is now, and there is no other way. We have to accept it.

Loving the present works well with another Thought, focusing on the positive (See Thought #2). If you overslept and missed an important meeting, then you can still make the best of your present situation. Feeling fully rested, you can apologize for arriving late and commit to doing your work duties to the best of your ability for the day. If you are ill or in pain, then you can still make the best of your present situation. The pain is your body sending loving signals to you, to help you heal yourself by guiding you to *not* do whatever it is that is causing you pain. If you are tired and miserable, and the day seems to be never-ending with things you must do, then you can still make the best of your present situation. Learn to see this as a loving test from the present, to see what you are truly capable of.

The present isn't trying to bring us misery, just as the child who does something wrong is not trying to bring us misery. The present and the child are just being. We interpret everything as good or bad, and this makes it so. Even death, something most of us would be scared to think about going through, can be reframed in the present moment. Dying can be a quest or a journey, an overcoming of all pains, an opportunity to truly rest and sleep deeply, to reflect on all of our life and its meaning, to forgive, to discover what truly happens after death. It is a chance to meet our loved ones or important religious figures, or a chance to become an angelic figure and watch over others who we care about. Also, it may be the ultimate opportunity to let go of everything – to let go of all the things we thought we needed, but never really did.

Learn to love the present. Learn to love and accept everything as it happens, because there is no better way to live. When the child does something wrong, we do not stop loving him. When the present does something that wrongs us, why would we stop loving it? The present will bring us happiness and miseries, and we have to learn to flow along with the tides and accept these things as they happen. Do not misunderstand. We can of course take control when possible, but often, the present brings many things that are not in our control. Therefore, it makes more sense to learn to accept things as they happen. We have to learn to stop needing to fix the things that ultimately were not even broken to begin with. Many of the wrongs we see in life are just things that didn't happen as we would have liked or expected. But this doesn't make them wrong to the universe. The universe allowed them to happen. Accept what is and let go of the need to have everything go in the way you would have liked.

Live Your Dream

Many of us have a dream, something we have always wanted to do, but we often have reasons or excuses as to why we can't do it yet. It's not the right time, we don't have the money, we don't have the training or the ability. The right time never seems to come, we never seem to have the money, and we never seem to find the opportunity to get trained and acquire the necessary abilities. It doesn't happen now. It doesn't happen ever. Then the dream slips away into a figment of our imaginations and it becomes harder to grasp, like trying to remember what you dreamed the night before, in the middle of the day. Eventually, maybe you even forget about it, accepting that it was never likely to happen.

One of my favorite quotes is this:

"People are capable at any time in their lives, of doing what they dream of." – *The Alchemist*, by Paulo Coelho

Is there ever really a reason to keep putting off your dreams, until later and later and later? Understand that it is an epic tragedy when you do not live out your dream. In truth, we have the chance in our lives to live out many dreams. Unfortunately, many of us will fail to fulfill even one.

What is your dream? When thinking about it, remember Thought #1, and phrase it in a way where you focus on things that are *within* your control. Your dream could be to write a novel, *not* necessarily to write a bestselling novel. Your dream may be to act in a film, *not* necessarily in a Hollywood production. Or your dream may be to finish a marathon, *not* necessarily to finish in first place. Understand that when you want something out of your control, and you have no plan, then that is a fantasy, not a dream.

As a real-life example, my wife always had the dream to live in Europe. And many years ago, I realized that my dream was to take a break from everything and to do nothing but read for a few years. We both realized that if we waited for the right time or the right situation to live out these dreams, that we may be waiting until retirement – which is decades away for us. In the worst case, we may never have lived them out.

Soon after discovering that my dream was to take a break from everything and to read, I realized that I had the power to do this *Now*. I didn't need to stop working or stop everything else in my life. If I simply organized my time, I could read plenty of books in a year. When I made up my mind to live my dream in the present, I started reading 40-50 books per year, and I have kept this pace year after year. Before making up my mind to do it, I was reading very few books— I was busy with work and I had neglected my dream.

Remember this: Things change instantly when you make up your mind to change them.

As my wife's dream was to live in Europe, as soon as it became possible she applied for work in some European countries, and ultimately she got a contract to work in Paris for three years. This is where we live as I write this book. Again, there was no reason to wait for a perfect time or for a perfect situation. We went to live in Europe at the first opportunity that we had.

I hear people talk about their dreams all the time. They want to start a business, invent something, write a book, travel the world, be a well-read person, or something else. Of course, when you ask them what the next step is, or what the plan is, they rarely have one. In many cases, I have heard complaints, explaining why it can't be done (See Thought #3), on how many people have tried and failed, or on why it's someone else's fault.

We tend to make the task of living out our dream bigger in our minds than it needs to be. Your dream gets stuck into being a big fantasy that needs to happen perfectly. Forget about perfection. Remember, I didn't end up dropping everything to live my dream as I originally wanted to. Instead, I decided to keep living my life just as I had been, and to build up my dream all at the same time. It wasn't as fantastical this way, but now I get to live my dream every day. It was as simple as picking up a book and reading a page.

You need to focus on the reality, on the present moment. Don't let your mind get too lost in *la la land*, or it may fly away and never come back to actually live the dream.

Ask yourself: *What is the next step to making my dream come true?* Is it writing a page? Is it learning to use a paintbrush? Is it taking a class in computer programming? Whatever it is, work on that, bit by bit. You may not see your dream come true today or tomorrow. But there is something you can do right now to get closer to making that dream happen. Do that. If money is an issue, find free resources, barter, or network with the people who are in a position to help you.

Fear of failure is a big obstacle to living the dream. For this reason, I don't recommend talking so much about your dream as I recommend living it. Many of the people I know who don't live their dream actually talk about it a lot. They spend more time talking about the dream than they do pursuing it, oddly enough. Do you know someone who is always telling you about their fantastic book idea, but strangely enough they aren't publishing? When we talk too much, we become even more fearful of failure. By building up ideas, we feel that we need to impress people. Really, impressing people is the wrong focus. Get as far away from that as you can. Talk less and take more action. Living the dream happens through action. These are small daily actions that happen moment by moment.

Remember this: Keep the dream alive. Feed the dream, and the dream will feed you.

Exercises

Practice mindfulness

Mindfulness means that you practice being in the present, being fully aware. It is not being stuck in your own mind, worrying about what you have to do later, or dwelling on the past. To me, the best place to be mindful is with nature. Go outside and appreciate nature for what it is, rather than treating it as an irrelevant background. To help build up a habit of mindfulness, I would advise starting with practicing it for one minute per day, then five minutes, then ten minutes, and keep building up gradually as you are able to. This will help to improve your focus, clarity, and feelings of peace and joy. Don't just be alive. Live.

Say this to yourself: What I am doing right now is worth all of my attention, energy, and commitment. If it is not, I must stop doing it and do that thing which is indeed worth all of my attention, energy, and commitment.

Avoid the fragmented mind that tries to be everywhere and therefore ends up going nowhere. Find that one thing that is truly worth your time and energy and do that with all of your mind and heart. Then, do the next thing which is worth all of your time and energy. Allow yourself the time to get fully into the zone of what you are doing. Do not feel rushed, moving from one trivial task to the next. Find meaning in your present moment and live it mindfully.

Create a physical trigger to remind you to stay in the present moment

On the #AskGaryVee show, Gary Vaynerchuk had an interview with Jewel. She talked about having a rough childhood, moving out of her home at 15 and being homeless by 18, while of course she ended up becoming a famous singer-songwriter by 21 years old. She said that one of the techniques she used to help her get over anxiety and panic attacks was to focus her mind on the present moment. Jewel admitted that this was not always easy, and something that helped her was to follow her hands and pay attention to them, to stay in the present. For you, you could observe your hands, listen to the wind, or you could stop and smell the roses. You can find anything to do – and just use that as a reminder to stay in the present moment. It helps if this is something that is common and naturally draws your attention to it.

If you find yourself in conversations about the distant past or future, try to guide them back to the present

Of course, if you have conversations with an older person, it is natural for them to recall more past events. However, when speaking with people your own age, aim to have more conversations that focus on the present. What is happening presently in people's lives? For the sake of conversation, the present can be broader than just the immediate moment, perhaps such as what has happened in the prior week, and what you are looking forward to in the coming week. When it comes to the distant past – we should have already learned the lessons that we needed to from it, and when it comes to the distant future, we tend to create fantasies. Focusing on the now keeps us based in a practical reality, and we are better able to appreciate our ability to control and guide our lives in the direction that we would like.

When you have a conversation, be fully present

When we speak with people and have conversations, we often struggle to be present, just as we struggle throughout much of the day. If someone is telling a story, we may be reminded about a different story that involved us and want to tell it, causing the mind to shift away from the present. We may be worried about what we are going to do later. Or we may see someone doing something interesting and become distracted from the conversation. It is important that we train ourselves to listen intently, to fully grasp what is being said and to understand it deeply.

Look at the person you are speaking with, observe her facial expressions, pay attention to the individual words used, and allow yourself to feel what this person is feeling. Process whether the tones are sad, uplifting, funny, or suspenseful. Tell yourself that you are in the right place, talking to the right person, and that this is all that matters right now.

THOUGHT #6

Focus on What You Need, *Not* on What You Want

"Distinguish between real needs and artificial wants and control the latter." – Mahatma Gandhi

From What You Have, Focus on What You Need

You may think that this Thought is quite similar to *Focus on what you have, not on what you do not have*, but upon reflection, I realized that this Thought is distinct and still important to include. The main issue with *only* focusing on what you have is that some people may have access to enormous amounts of wealth – and focusing on what they have may not be especially useful in such cases. There is nothing wrong with having wealth, but as with power, with great wealth comes great responsibility. For the person who already has an abundance, focusing on needs will be more important to clarifying what is truly important in her life. Even for the person who does not have an abundance, focusing on needs will help to prioritize what truly matters and what is most important to pursue or to preserve in life.

I believe this thought will be the one that meets the most resistance for many readers. We have gotten used to feeling that we need more and more. But perhaps these feelings are not based in reality. Perhaps we don't need everything that we think we do.

The media, the people we know, and the culture are all telling us that we need more things to be happy. We need vacations. We need more friends. We need more fancy products to make our lives a little bit easier.

We use the word "need" so loosely, that much of the time when people use it, you can assume that they mean "want."

Something to be cautious about is that we tend to get addicted to the attention we receive from the things we have but don't need. Years ago, an acquaintance I knew had just bought a massive stereo system for his pickup truck. The sound system was so big that it took up the back seats in the truck, with no room for anyone to sit there. He was showing it off to his friends and me. His friends were complimenting him on how great it was, and how much they wished they could get something like it for themselves. I didn't say much about it, but my thought was that this was completely unnecessary. Was he *that* much happier with this sound system than he would have been with a more modest one? A sound system like this used at its full power would likely lead to deafness. He would often purchase exaggerated items of this sort, that were so big and expensive that his friends were amazed, and they would shower him with attention. I sensed that this acquaintance became addicted to the attention, despite that he didn't need any of these items.

When many of us have so much, perhaps a more important question to ask ourselves is: *What do we really need? And, are we meeting all of those needs, or is there something lacking in our lives?*

Visualize Your Perfect Life in Great Detail

I would like you to do a quick exercise with me.

Visualize your perfect life. Spare no expense, as money is not an issue. You can rearrange the whole planet in any way you wish. How much money would you have in your bank account? How big would your home be? How much food would you have in the refrigerator? Where would you go on vacation? Who would your spouse be? How many perfectly behaved children would you have? How exotic would your car collection or rare arts collection be? What special technologies would you have access to? Think about it. Imagine it in detail.

When you have finished, I want you to realize that you don't need any of this. Does it really make you more fulfilled to have these things, or is it more fulfilling to seek it out and work for it yourself? Remember what I said earlier: using cheat codes is completely unfulfilling. The path, the process, and the moment are the answer to life's questions, not achieving some end state.

When you realize that you don't need all of the perfect outcomes given to you, and that if it were offered to you, you should turn it down, life will open up some amazing opportunities to you. You will start to enjoy the trials and tribulations that come your way, because they will become a part of your personal quest.

We all go to the movies and read books about people who go on great quests and adventures, and we admire them. It only makes sense that the ideal life would mimic these tales in a way – obviously, perhaps with less life-threatening dangers. I would like you to understand that the ideal life is not retirement from life itself. The ideal life is the journey that you take while you are seeking your best life. This is not given to you – it is pursued with a great personal drive. When you are pursuing your ideal life whole-heartedly, this is when you are already living it.

What Would You *Need* to Be Truly Fulfilled?

This time, I have a different question for you. *What would you need to be truly fulfilled?* Think of where you would work, where you would live, who you would be accompanied by, the things you would own, the things you would do....

Envision what your good life would mean – not the perfect life, but just good, just happy. If you know exactly what you *need* for this, and work every day in steps to get there, it will be much more achievable. Perhaps you are already there.

In creating this good life, be sure to remove the things which are not necessary, which do not truly contribute to your growth, happiness, or betterment in some way. Identify the things that are most necessary to meet your goals, and get rid of the rest, to illuminate the shortest path to the good life.

Next, consider this question: *What would you need to feel happy?* Any wants above this that cost you too much to acquire in time, life, and energy will bring less happiness, not more. Remember that these should be things that help you to get the maximum enjoyment out of the present moment.

I find that the more minimal I keep my needs and wants, the happier I am. If you feel that you must have all of these extravagant things, you may one day find that you are miserable unless you wake up in your mansion, and your personal chef cooks you the most exotic and expensive meals from around the world. If you cannot have this, then you cannot bear to even get up in the morning. It seems silly, but this is the direction we move toward every time we tell ourselves that we need to have some unnecessary thing or that otherwise we will be miserable. Our thinking it makes it true.

If you find yourself slipping in that direction, feeling that you need more and more conveniences, occasionally you should have a day where you restrain yourself. Rather than going out to eat or ordering food, you would make something quick with whatever you happen to have in the fridge. You may actually choose to fast for a half day or for a day – assuming your doctor approves. This will remind you that not only do you *not* need fancy foods, you don't need food as much as you thought at all. Something else that you could do is instead of taking your vehicle to work, you could take public transportation for a day.

To go a step further, if you feel that you could benefit from having a wider perspective, then spend some time around people who have very little. Volunteer at a homeless shelter or talk with a homeless person on the street to learn what his life is like. Instead of worrying about what name brand his clothing is, he'll have other concerns – mainly about what he truly needs just to survive.

The above exercises are meant to show you the difference between what you think you need and what you truly need. Also of course, they will help you to become filled with gratitude, rather than with concern over any insignificant wants that you may have.

The Great Costs of Pursuing Wants Over Needs

Consider this scenario:

John decides to buy a house that his wife, son and daughter do not need, but they want it badly. It has a swimming pool, a massive backyard, and it is in the best neighborhood in his city. The cost was immense and soon after paying the down payment, he worries if he will be able to afford it. Then other troubles begin – he is surprised to find that the house needs some repairs which are quite expensive. Soon enough, John is disappointed to find that he does not have enough money for anything extra such as vacations or shopping money, or even for entertainment. The entire focus becomes keeping the house at all costs.

He decides to work overtime at his regular job during the night, and he takes an extra job mowing lawns on the weekends – meaning all of his time is used for work rather than actually enjoying the home or spending time with family. Regardless of what he does to earn more money, there is a constant pressure, stress, and fear that it will not be enough. This is the home that his family lives in. Everyone is attached to it, and if he were to lose the house, he would feel like a failure. John begins having frequent nightmares and occasional panic attacks. He gains weight as he only has time to eat junk food, and his general health and mental health decline through the years. He has the house for now, but he will always be worried about losing it until the day it is paid off.

In the story above, John has kept the house, but if his health continues to deteriorate or if he is unlucky and loses his job, he could easily lose the house in the coming years. Furthermore, with all of the stress and lack of time spent with his wife and family, a divorce is much more likely to occur. Remember that certain purchases are so big that if we are not careful, they have the potential to ruin us. This is the cost of pursuing wants over needs.

Our desires get us into trouble

Desiring new things that are placed in front of you makes you vulnerable to aggressive marketers or even scammers who may call you, advertise to you, or stop you on the street with a "fantastic new product." Likely, they will point out a problem that had not been especially bothersome to you before, but the elite salesperson will try to make you see how much you really "need" what they are selling. You are more likely to be taken advantage of by such tactics when you want new things that you don't truly need. My rule of thumb for staying out of trouble in such situations is to refuse to make a decision in the moment. The salesperson will do everything in their power to get you to buy now, and slash prices – which should only prove the point that what they are selling is not worth it. If you inform them of your rule that you do not make decisions in the moment, then they will find it hard to argue with that, and you can leave the situation.

Freedom, a Need That is Often Overlooked

As humans we have a need for freedom, something that is perhaps taken for granted now. There are different kinds of freedom. Some examples are to have the freedom to think what you want, to say what you want, and to do what you want. Of course, there are normally some restrictions as defined by our laws. And these restrictions are usually to keep people safe, so that your freedoms do not allow you to say or take actions that cause other people harm.

Ask anyone and they will agree that freedom is important. But sometimes we live as if it were not. If you restrict your freedom because you are pursuing too many wants, then you have to ask if these wants of yours are really worth the price of your freedom. Understand that wanting more, and pursuing more wants, tends to take your time and freedom away. Strangely enough, many people admit to working a job that they don't even like. They started off in a job they didn't like in the pursuit of money to buy the things they thought they needed, the "false needs." Then they got trapped, they lost their freedom and became *Slaves of Wants*.

Slaves of Wants have become trapped by their wants, no longer having the freedom to do what they want with their life, trapped either by prior false needs and their costs, or by the wish of future false needs that they were unwilling to let go of. This entrapment can be especially vicious in the modern age, where it is easy to rack up massive amounts of debt, which can keep us in the Slave of Wants position for perhaps a lifetime. Recall the story of John earlier and his unfortunate purchase of a home that was too expensive. He became a Slave of Wants.

> "We buy things we don't need with money we don't have to impress people we don't like." – from *Fight Club* by Chuck Palahniuk

To make matters even worse than the quote above suggests, sometimes we *work for a boss we can't stand at a job we don't like* to "buy things we don't need with money we don't have to impress people we don't like." Of course, this is the worst-case scenario, but for many people, it will ring true. In such cases, we should stop and ask ourselves: *What am I doing? Is there a better way? If I simply wanted less and focused on my needs would that help to fix the problem? Should I have searched for a job that I was happy with, rather than going straight to the job that paid the most, but left me miserable?*

Why are there so many people with so many *false needs* – which are basically wants? My theory is that for our evolutionary history, humans have required stress for survival. Those who did not stress at all were so carefree that they may have been easy prey for a tiger, and so they would not pass on their genes. Those who stressed, worried about tigers, and so they stayed alert and were a lot more likely to see the tiger before the tiger saw them, and to find a way to stay safe and survive. Of course, those who survived were likely to pass on their genes. Thus, we are all predisposed to some level of stress, and if our stress level is too low, we create false needs, so that we have something to stress over. Even if we need these levels of stress, which is debatable, there are better ways to go about it. For example, we may pursue a challenging activity, exercise, socialize, or something else to pursue a good kind of stress. Understand why you create the false need, and then the feeling that you *need* it may just go away.

Personally, I play chess. When I have nothing else to do, instead of allowing myself to feel stressed over something I want, I play this game. Through chess, I challenge myself to improve in my skills, which provides a different, good kind of stress. If this game doesn't interest you, that is fine. Find some other type of challenge to work on to occupy your mind. Occupy your mind with something positive of your choosing, such as with learning something new, or it will tend to become occupied with things that don't matter, with pursuits that cause you harm.

If You Want to Know What You Really Need...

According to Abraham Maslow, an American psychologist who studied human motivations and needs, there is a *hierarchy of needs*. This means that there are basic needs that people will have to meet first before they can attain higher level needs. I like to separate the needs that he proposes in terms of *needs for survival* and *needs to thrive*. Of course, needs for survival are those that you absolutely need just to survive and to feel safe in your day to day life. Needs to thrive are deep needs that we have in order to do well in life, and to be able to reach our potential.

To regain a focus and ability to prioritize what is truly important in life, consider Maslow's hierarchy of needs below.

Needs to survive

Physiological needs – includes breathing, water, food, sleep, clothing, shelter.

These are the most basic needs where if most of us did not have access to them, modern civilization as we know it could not exist. In today's world, most people will be able to have these basic needs met in return for providing a service to society – usually in the form of a job. Even for those without a job, most of these are generally viewed as a human right, and many governments will have programs to help people who cannot afford these basic needs.

Safety – includes personal security, emotional security, financial security, health and well-being, and safety against accidents or illness.

Again, being safe and feeling safe is something that is critical to everyday society. When most people do not feel safe or that what they own is safe, it is difficult to have a functioning community. The foundations of society are based on order and predictability, and one of the most important parts of having order is to feel that you can expect to be safe, and not be harassed or attacked or stolen from at any moment.

Social belonging – includes love, friendship, intimacy, and family.

Love and feelings of belonging may not seem essential for survival. It's easy to see that lack of food and water or being attacked can be highly problematic to your survival, but so can a lack of social belonging. Throughout the history of humanity, we have been social creatures that have relied on each other for help. One of the great strengths of the human species is not our physical strength or speed, where many other species easily surpass us. Our strength is in using the power of the mind to solve problems and to invent what we need to help us to solve problems. Through our ability to communicate with one another, we are able to *magnify the power of the mind* to arrive at better solutions than we could have arrived at independently.

Beyond the practicality of belonging to a group such as family, a work team, a community, a country, etc., social belonging is critical to our mental, physical, and spiritual health. As humans, we feel a deep need for love and to communicate with one another, and this is something that may not become evident unless we are thrust into a situation where we do not belong anywhere. Suddenly, there is no one to ask for help even for something basic. There is no one to listen to your life's problems, and it seems like you are alone in the world and you feel hopeless. As with many of our needs, the best way to understand their importance is to imagine how life would be if suddenly they disappeared from our lives. Douglas Nemecek, the chief medical officer at Cigna has said: "Loneliness has the same impact on mortality as smoking 15 cigarettes a day, making it even more dangerous than obesity." This further supports just how important it is to develop and cultivate our real-life social connections.

Needs to thrive

Esteem – this is the need to be respected and valued.

This includes both the need to feel respect from others, and the need to have self-respect. To see the importance of esteem, consider someone who has a low self-esteem, and a low confidence. This is someone who will feel that he is not worthy of success, that he is not worthy of having a good life, and because of this belief, he is unlikely to achieve what he wants in life. He will easily accept a life that is not meeting his needs. This person may become more attracted to groups of people who also think negatively, and ultimately, they may all drag each other down into a troubled way of life.

In contrast, a person with high esteem will feel good, will feel that he is capable of accomplishing what he wishes to accomplish. He will not back down from a challenge because he will feel capable of overcoming this. I believe that esteem is generally achieved after having met all of the *Needs to survive* that were listed above. If you have all of your basic survival needs met, along with having a sense of social belonging, then you will have every reason to feel good and confident about yourself. The world will seem like a positive place, and so you will feel positive about yourself.

Self-actualization – a person's motivation and ability to reach his or her potential.

Again, once all of the prior needs have been met, you will have the ideal conditions to pursue your true potential. Once you have met all of your prior needs, you may think: *I have plenty of food, I live in a good and safe neighborhood, I have love in my life, and I have a steady income from my work. What now?*

When you have a very good life, you will be in a position to become philosophical and ask questions. Some people may ask, *Is this really all there is?* They may feel frustrated, and this is where some people mistakenly begin the pursuit of more and more money or stuff. This becomes the purpose, because there is no other clear purpose set out for them. However, it is more important to pursue the *happy, peaceful, and meaningful life*.

Pursuing self-actualization may involve putting all of your energy into learning about a topic, perhaps pursuing a degree, and continuing to educate yourself to become one of the best in your field. Note that the people who pursue their own actualization often end up providing some of the greatest outcomes for the public. They may provide hundreds of jobs to workers and create products that help solve problems, for example. Also, often enough the people who produce greatly end up having created such an excess for themselves that they will donate some of it back to the public. The point here is that there is a relationship between self-actualization or becoming your best self, and helping society at large. Thus, if society and civilization have a goal, it seems clear that the goal should be to create as many self-actualized individuals as is possible.

Everyone Has Wants – and They Are Not the Enemy, Unless We Let Them Spiral out of Control

I have wants, as I'm sure everyone does. But even with my wants, I split them into two main categories to avoid having them spiral out of control.

Generally, wants that in some way support your needs to survive and thrive are much more valuable than wants that are strictly for entertainment. For example, if you have a full wardrobe of clothing, it's doubtful that you truly *need* some new item of clothing. But, perhaps rather than wearing your three worn out old coats for winter, it would make more sense to just buy a new high quality one. It is sensible to have good quality clothing, we just have to be cautious about feeling that we always need to wear something new and trendy – in that case we may have a problem.

Another common item I would buy that isn't essential to survival, but quite helpful to thriving, would be books. I generally don't restrain myself from these purchases because I know that the knowledge and understanding I acquire will help me to thrive. Learn not to feel guilty for such small and resourceful purchases – provided of course that you have the funds available.

I am also open to making purchases that in some way support others' needs to survive and thrive – if a family member or friend told me that he was raising money to take a course so he could learn to setup his own business, this is something that I would consider helping out with.

Wants that are strictly for your own personal enjoyment are fine, as we should all enjoy ourselves, but since these wants don't fulfill a higher role or purpose, I try to limit them. These can turn into addictions if you are not careful. Of course, these would be wants such as buying new shoes, a new TV, a new car, etc. If an old item has broken and it was important to me, however, I am normally fine with repairing or replacing it.

Whenever I am going to purchase something, I always consider – *How much am I actually going to use this item, and how long will it last me, compared to how much it costs?* For this reason, I am not too concerned with paying a fairly large amount for a laptop – because I know it should last me about 5 years and that I use it a lot for my work. On the other hand, I would not be interested in spending any money for a CD player, because I rarely find the need to listen to an actual CD – I tend to stream my music instead. Even if the CD player were at a great bargain, I would not buy it because I know that I would not use it. If I know that I will use an item rarely, I may prefer to buy it at a discount, to borrow the item, or even rent it if that is an option.

Consider that everything we own comes at a cost. Eventually, things break and need repairs. Often, the repair costs are a great nuisance and some people will just upgrade and buy an even more expensive replacement. Some items require ongoing maintenance, subscription fees, or you must buy extra equipment just to make good use of what you bought. Otherwise, you may need to spend some time cleaning or dusting off the things that you accumulate. Be careful with acquiring so many unnecessary items that they get in your way and prevent you from moving forward in your life.

Generally, I am minimalistic preferring to own less items, but have them be items that I truly need or want, and I will own high quality versions of those things. When I see an item of interest, my first question to myself is always – *Do I need this?* If I can avoid making a purchase, I usually do. This is because items accumulate quickly, and we tend to forget about all of the old items we have already purchased. We tend to have the problem of having too much that we don't need, rather than not having enough of what we need.

I have seen many instances of people purchasing items that were unimportant and unnecessary, which would leave me wondering if there was not something more necessary that they could have spent this on. In the majority of cases, there was indeed something more critical that had been completely overlooked or neglected. Sometimes it was health – doctor's visits were completely ignored. Sometimes it was education – staying stuck in an undesirable job instead of pursuing a path forward. Other times it was a basic cleaning service – continuing to live in a messy space instead of having it cleaned up. A new gadget would often provide a distraction from what was truly important, making things worse, not better.

Instead of always seeking new *things* in your life, consider the value of forming new *experiences* as well. Remember that through experiences, you tend to grow, learn, bond with people, and build new interesting memories.

Again, wants are not the enemy. Everyone has wants, and everyone gives in to them sometimes. I just ask that we exercise some caution and always remember our priorities. The issue is that some people spend so much time and energy taking care of their wants that they forget what their needs truly were, leaving them in a perpetual unbalanced and unfulfilled state.

Remember this: Before we focus on our wants, we must take a step back and ask what it is that we really need.

What do You *Need* to Do in Your Day to Day Life?

The things that we *need* to do most are often the things that we *want* to do the least. This means that if we are not highly organized, we will always be tempted to do fun and easy tasks, rather than work on the things that we need to be doing – usually the more challenging and unpleasant tasks.

I would like to introduce you to my system to help you prioritize your life by what you really need to do. Every week I organize my Master To-Do List, where I write down everything that I need to do. I will show you how to do this now.

Like most people, I have many different components to my life, however, there is a basic priority of needs that I always aim to keep in mind. For example, major family concerns always come first. If there is a major problem that needs to be taken care of with myself or anyone in my family, helping with this will become my first priority. Next, I focus on necessary life tasks – paying bills, paying taxes, doctor's visits, getting groceries, ordering an important book or item online, and so forth.

After this, I focus on my work. Since work is such a large aspect of our lives, I would strongly advise breaking up your work into components. Break up your work tasks into 3-7 categories, and then rank them in order of importance. This will make your life much easier. Instead of just having a general Work category, I have major categories such as Home Life, Main Project, Distribution & Expansion, General Business Tasks & Miscellaneous, and Future Book Projects [**I bold these headings** on the actual list]. Of course, some home life tasks will not be so important, but in general, my home life is the most critical part of my life. This includes groceries, buying medicine for myself or a family member, and running important errands. After this, I will also create subcategories to further organize each section [*I italicize these subheadings* on the actual list], and I will organize those by importance as well. Lastly, you can list out all of the tasks you need to do under the relevant category. Aim to organize them by need or importance, but do not stress over how you rank items that are similarly important.

All of this may seem like a great deal of work, but if you stop most people on the street and ask them what they *need* to do today, they may not have a good answer. They can show you some tasks they have written down, but it's unlikely to be put in order of what they truly need to do.

I regularly have anywhere from 30-50 items to take care of, and I make special efforts to remove those which are not actually necessary. If they are not organized in some way by what needs to be done, I will waste a lot of time figuring out what to do first. As much time as it seems like it would take to make a Master To-Do list, it is fully worthwhile. It may take you an hour to create your list. However, it may only take 10 minutes to update it once per week. For me, it is much easier to do this in an online file, so I can easily edit and make changes without needing to rewrite a full list every week.

As an additional tip – when you have many tasks you are working on, it is easy to forget the status of an incomplete item. For that reason, I will often write a note when I am waiting to make progress on a task. For example, if I am waiting for someone's response to an important message, I would note that I am waiting for a response from this person and what the date is. I will highlight such status updates in yellow, so I can see them at a glance. If you know that you will want to check in on the status of something later, you may write, "Check in with [person] by [date] if I have not heard anything back."

I find it helpful to include deadlines next to my tasks, especially if I notice that some tasks have been on my list for weeks without having made any progress. Some tasks have actual deadlines that you need to meet, but if a true deadline does not exist, it is useful to create one for yourself to help ensure that you complete the task.

In addition to this, I will then put the items that I intend to work on for the week into Google Calendar (it's free to use). It is fully worth learning how to use the features of this app, as you can put in repeating time slots, which is useful if you always have a meeting at the same time every week. I recommend making general descriptions for your tasks in your calendar. Your specific tasks are already written on your To-Do list, so there is no need to clutter your calendar with them. To keep things simple, I will typically only have one scheduled block for the morning, and one for the evening. If I have a meeting or something that needs to be done at a specific time, I will highlight that block in red. If you feel like this is too simple, then feel free to add extra blocks into your calendar. Keep in mind that if you are working on tasks, or sets of tasks that are truly important and necessary, then wouldn't it make more sense to spend several hours on them? However, everyone has different needs. Do what works best for you.

Some people advise only having a calendar and not to bother with To-Do lists, but I find the To-Do list to be critical. When you have 20+ items to work on for the week that are not trivially easy, prioritizing them becomes important. Writing them down in a Master To-Do list *is* the way to prioritize them. Some people may also ask, *Why would you bother having a calendar when your To-Do list tells you everything?* For me, it is also critical to have a calendar because looking at a Master To-Do List that is several pages long can feel overwhelming. I feel much better looking at a clear and organized calendar that tells me what I should be doing, and when I should be doing it. I can also feel good in knowing that it has already been organized by priority, according to the necessity and importance of my To-Do items. I can simply flip back to my To-Do list if I need a reminder of the specific tasks that needed to be done.

I have experimented extensively with how I organize my To-Do items and my calendar, and this is what I have found to be the most effective and efficient system for organizing my life priorities. It works because it takes into account what truly needs to be done. The mind wants to do what it wants, not what it needs, so we must find organizational systems that always keep our minds on what needs to be done.

Put some time into thinking about what tasks you do and why you do them. Ask if they are truly necessary. You may find that some tasks you thought were important don't actually matter much. Understand that mindlessly performing tasks is not efficiency. Thinking about what you truly have to do and then doing those things in order of priority is true efficiency.

Needs Above Wants

Ultimately, you decide what you need in your life. For one person, love may be lacking. For another, there may be a tremendous ambition to live up to her full capabilities. Another person may need to provide food and shelter for his family. Understand that you alone get to decide what *needs* to be done. Often in our lives, we have many people telling us what we need to do, but sometimes they are imposing their own needs onto you. Some of those needs may be things we agree with, and some not. Be sure to focus on those things that you agree are your true needs.

Understand that *need* is a powerful word. When you *want* something, you are willing to work months or maybe a year to make it happen. You are willing to set goals to pursue it. But if something else more important happens, or if there are too many obstacles in your path, you drop it. At the end of the day, a want is just a want. With needs on the other hand, you may be willing to work all day every day to get them, and you may be willing to suffer greatly. Due to the importance of our needs, you may even be willing to die for them – for example, the need to protect your child. Needs have a truly powerful effect on us.

Some people may feel like they have many wants, but few real needs. In modern society, our basic survival needs are often met easily. However, our creative, emotional, and spiritual needs are often lacking. When you decide that some of your personal needs are not really needs, that they are not important, and that your wants are more important, this is truly a dark path to go down. Just because something is not required for survival, does not mean that it is not a need. If you need something to feel happy, fulfilled, at peace, and that you are on the path to living your best and most meaningful life, then it is a need. Forget about those wants that are in fact probably getting in the way of your needs.

Let's consider some statistics. According to Neilsen, the average American watches five hours of TV per day. Meanwhile, various surveys online have shown that the average time spent on social media sites is two hours per day. This means that seven hours per day are wasted for most people. I feel safe in using this estimate, because I have not even considered other common time-wasters – I have only focused on two of the major ones. This is time that could be used doing any number of things that would fulfill our greater needs – our needs to express our creativity, emotions, spirituality, love, to live our purpose, or even to go on a personal quest.

My point here is not to make you feel lousy for wasting some time. We all need time to relax and refresh, but this can become excessive and pointless. And I know many people who lie to themselves – claiming they don't have time to pursue their dream, when they are burning up that time every day.

What I wish to make you understand is that until you identify your core human needs, and put those on a pedestal above everything else, they will not be met. You will perpetually get stuck in trying to find temporary satisfaction from meeting wants. But that doesn't work. The human mind is built to take the easy path – and going after those wants is the easy way. If you can just buy something right now that appears to solve a problem, that is easy. We all do it. In reality, it doesn't solve anything – it's usually just a distraction from meeting your true needs.

You must identify your core human needs, and then make up your mind that even if these are not necessary for survival, that they are *your* needs – and this makes them important. Your true meaning is in your needs, in fulfilling them. Write down your response to this question: *What are all of your human needs, in order, and then what are all of the wants that are in fact just obstacles to meeting those needs?* When you are ready, if you find that some of those wants are major obstacles to your needs, you may get rid of them, or at least stop allowing them into your life.

Remember this: Choose your needs above your wants, or you will get to have your wants without having met your true needs.

When Your Needs are Met, What Then?

If this chapter of the book has had its intended effect, I hope that you may find that you actually already have everything that you need right now. An interesting question to ask after that is, "What does the world need?" This isn't meant to be a question about saving the world, instead, it's about asking what you can do to help others, or what you can do to help animals, or other life on the planet. What is your part that you could do, even if it is small? Just think about it. We should always keep in mind that even if we have all of our needs met, that there are plenty of people out there who have not attained this yet.

Exercises

Create your Master To-Do List

Before you begin, I recommend using a Word file so that you can make modifications to your master To-Do list more easily. When you are ready, ask yourself what the main categories of your life are. If you have full time work with many different responsibilities, you may use more than one main category for your work. If you are a parent, then **Parenting** may be its own category, to make sure your kids' needs are being met. **Household Tasks** could be another category, which could include subcategories such as *Cleaning, Organizing,* and *Vacation Planning*.

If you have personal goals that do not relate to your work or home life, this could be a separate category as well. For example, a personal goal could be to make new friends, learn to cook, or to get more exercise. Put your **Main Categories in bold**. Then, if you have a large list of tasks that you need to do, I recommend creating *Subcategories in italics*. For example, if you have a main category that is **Meetings**, you may actually have *General Meetings, Research Meetings,* and *Educational Meetings* that you must go to. These could be your subcategories.

After you have determined all of your **Main Categories** and their *Subcategories,* write in all of your tasks. The larger your list, the more important it is to keep your tasks only to important things that need to be done. Example tasks for the Parenting category could involve picking up your kids from school, to help plan their summer activities, and to take them to the zoo. I put the check box icon [☐] in front of my tasks. You can print off your list and check them off through the week if you like. Lastly, make sure that your main categories are prioritized in order. Then make sure that all of your subcategories are also prioritized in order. Then, also check to make sure that your tasks are listed in order of priority.

Update your Master To-Do List weekly, and then plan your week by scheduling it in Google Calendar, or another calendar if you prefer.

Which needs are being met in your life?

Remember to consider Maslow's Hierarchy of needs. *Physiological needs* include breathing, water, food, sleep, clothing, and shelter. *Safety needs* include personal security, emotional security, financial security, health and well-being, and safety against accidents or illness. *Social belonging needs* include love, friendships, intimacy, and family. *Esteem needs* include the need to be respected and valued. *Self-actualization* is a person's motivation and ability to reach his or her potential. Keep in mind that some of your needs may be partially fulfilled. If that is the case, consider what you would need to do to have them completely fulfilled.

For a week, or a month if you are determined, practice asking yourself if you truly need something whenever you are about to make a purchase

When you are going to make a purchase, ask yourself: *Do I really need this? Can I do everything I need to do without this item?* Remember that we create more and more *false needs* (e.g., things we feel that we need, but actually do not) as we get used to more and more conveniences. I would not wish to make you feel guilty about occasionally indulging in something that you want, especially inexpensive things, but we should reevaluate our lives when we are becoming obsessive and compulsive, often feeling the need to indulge in the things that we want. Keep in mind that often, those things serve no real need or larger purpose. They simply fill up space in our lives, sucking up our time, life, and energy.

Ask yourself what you need to do more of and need to focus more on

I have made great breakthroughs in my work by focusing deeply on what was needed. In the modern age it is easy to get distracted and to find something to work on that keeps you busy. But just because something keeps you busy doesn't mean that it is important. For any work or personal goals, there will often be many things that *need* to be done. These are needs because without them, big problems will tend to develop. When my mind is going in many different directions, and I feel like there is so much to do, I just calmly think about what it is that I *need* to do. Remember that what we need to do and want to do are often in conflict. However, if we take care of what needs to be done in the present, later on we will have more free time to do what we want.

Ask yourself if there is a need *not* being met in your life

We need to be careful not to become obsessed with wants and trivial things, forgetting about some real needs that we have. The needs that we have not met are sometimes obvious, such as if we find ourselves without a place to live. However, much of the time we will have all of our main survival needs met to a basic level, but our full needs will not be met. This can create anxiety and bitterness – as we feel like we are doing everything right but that there is still something missing.

These are some common needs that we may find missing from our lives: Love and kindness, respect, to pursue our true purpose, to find a companion, relaxation and peace, feeling free to be who we truly are, compassion, to love ourselves, emotional and spiritual fulfillment, to forgive and be forgiven, to have an outlet for our creativity, and to be free from our own self-created anguish.

Reflect deeply – perhaps in silence or in a meditative session and ask yourself what you need right now that is *not* being met. Understand that when it comes to having a healthy and fulfilled mind and spirit, we are not discussing wants – these are *needs*. If not cared for, the spirit can decay and wither away just as the body would if not cared for. Modern society mostly pays attention to the body and its health, but we tend to neglect our psychological, emotional, and spiritual well-being.

THOUGHT #7

Focus on What You Can Give, *Not* on What You Can Take

"You give but little when you give of your possessions. It is when you give of yourself that you truly give." – Kahlil Gibran

The Spirit of Giving

The prior Thought ended with reflections on what the world needs. Ask yourself: *What can I give to those who are in need?* If your basic needs to survive and thrive are not met, of course, do not worry about giving yet. This is something that can wait. But for those of us who realize that we already have what we need and much more, it may be a good time to think about what we can give.

You may have heard that sometimes people will say that you must give if you want to receive. I have read many quotes that say something like this, some even by quite prominent people, and although I agree that this is a true statement, it is the wrong focus. When we give, are we only giving because we hope to get something in return? Is this really the point? I don't think so. What we fail to realize is that the world has already given us plenty, and perhaps the fact that we are able to give is its own reward. Perhaps the fact that our lives are in balance, and that we have received an abundance, means that we should pass some of that abundance to those who could use it.

Feeling that *all* of our actions must benefit ourselves is selfish and keeps us stuck at a lower level of consciousness. When our needs are met, we must learn to move beyond the self, and to see that there is something much greater than just us in this world.

When I was growing up I would sometimes see an optometrist, and I discovered through chance that she would volunteer her time on Saturdays to help the people who could not afford her service. She would do this for no charge at a nonprofit institution. I realized that this was quite thoughtful and benevolent of her. Of course, people who could not afford her normal service also needed to have healthy eyes, and to have their vision corrected. Luckily for them, she was there.

Understand that you can give, and it does not need to be tangible, it does not need to be money. It can be time and skills that you give. If you see someone in need, you may find out what the problem is and try to provide her with that specific item. For instance, this can be as simple as if someone needs advice on an area where you have meaningful experience, then you could provide that advice. Otherwise, you may lend an item to someone who needs it, such as giving shoes or clothing.

The Gift within You is the One You Can Give to the World

If you have found a gift within you, this is what you are most capable of giving, without a need to always receive something in return for it. I believe everyone has a gift. However, you may not have discovered yours yet.

How do you know what your gift is?

If you often get compliments for your ability to do something, that may be your gift.

If you have done something naturally, and excelled at it since you were young, that may be your gift.

If you spend much of your time thinking about something, and you are happy to think about it and happy to do it, that may be your gift.

Despite that I am using the word *gift* you are not necessarily born with your gifts – you may have acquired them through a lot of work or experience. If you have a college degree in something, your gift may be related to your degree.

I would encourage you to think about your gifts deeply. Don't settle on the first obvious options that you think about. Keep thinking and you may just discover something new about yourself. Your gift may be for something that you thought was a fun waste of time, but perhaps it was not. Perhaps there is a way to turn that activity into something more meaningful. For example, you may be able to teach others how to do what you are gifted at.

There is surely something that comes naturally for you, but that is hard work and even a pain for others – this may be your gift.

To provide you with an example, my gifts are for listening, asking good questions, helping people, learning, and wisdom.

There are no rules for how to phrase your gifts. If my gifts seem quite broad and not very specific, it's because I like to use my gifts broadly. I like to learn in many, many areas. I listen very carefully to people, regardless of the problem they may have, and this then helps me to ask good questions that can help to resolve the problem. And all of these prior gifts help to contribute to my general wisdom.

Keep in mind that no one gets to tell you what your gifts are. If someone has an impression of you, then you can listen, but in the end, you get to decide. I might even suggest an experiment. If you think you have a major weakness, tell yourself that it is your gift, and you may be surprised that flipping this switch in your mind is all you need to turn one of your greatest weaknesses into one of your greatest strengths.

What Can All of us Give?

Many people will say, I have nothing to give. This is not true. We can all give something. Here, I will consider what some things are that we should all be able to give.

Acknowledgment

What is the worst punishment a human could receive? To be in prison, behind bars for life? I have always thought that this would be worse than death, because in death you suffer greatly for a short time, and then it is over. In prison, you would continue to suffer, day after day. But where do they send the prisoners who are too bad to be with the other prisoners? They send them to the SHU, which is solitary confinement. Here, you are invisible. No one acknowledges you as a person anymore. You are no longer a human being, just a thing taking up space.

The worst thing is to be invisible. This would mean that you do not matter, that you are irrelevant, and not worth acknowledging because you are not there. Imagine being treated in this way. Homeless people deal with this – no one knows quite what to do or say, so they just walk by and ignore them. Our elderly populations can become depressed, not because they are older, but because they are acknowledged less as human beings. They are sometimes seen as burdens that we take care of, rather than as someone with a spirit and soul.

In the African Zulu language, *Sawubona* means "I see you," and the response, *Ngikhona* means "I am here." This is a greeting that is said instead of what is used in most cultures "Hello, Hello," or "Good day, Good day." This means there is at least one culture that believes strongly in simply acknowledging our presence, the mere fact that we are here, right now.

I would encourage you to give the gift of acknowledging someone who has not been acknowledged.

Kindness

Every day, aim to do something helpful, give a compliment, send a thank you note, hold a door open, or ask someone if they could use some help. Just as anger and hatred can spread like wildfire, so can kindness, a power seldom used. If you see someone looking miserable, even if you do not know her, just smile, and ask "How are you?". If she says, "Not so good," then you can say "I'm sorry if it's not going so well. I hope things get better soon. I'm sure they will." You can politely excuse yourself after a moment, unless of course this person starts a conversation with you. The point is sometimes people are drowning in a negative state, and a small token of kindness can go a long way. You never know how much this might mean to this person. The last sentence I recommended, "I'm sure they will," is meant to plant a positive seed in the person – *Even this stranger who doesn't know me thinks everything might turn out well. Maybe there is a way for things to get better.*

Love

For someone you love, be sure to let this person know. If someone who you love is going through a difficult time, check in to make sure that this person is doing fine. Give a hug. Write a note for what you are grateful for about this person. For a chore that this person normally takes care of, help out and take care of it yourself. If this person you love is moving away, give a heartfelt and meaningful gift. Do not forget the ones you love, and do not allow them to think that they are not loved.

An ear to listen, not judge

Learn to understand when someone is very stressed and overwhelmed, in great pain. In such cases, you do not need to be overly rational and explain that they are wrong to see things the way they do. Realize that feelings cannot be wrong, and perspectives (e.g., points of view) cannot be wrong. They just are. In those times of great stress and turmoil, people need someone to listen and try to understand their situation. Sometimes people legitimately need a problem solved, and sometimes they are under a stressful pain, and the only thing that can relieve it is to have someone who will listen compassionately. After they have calmed down and the anxiety has eased, they may be ready for you to help them with the actual problem, in a nonjudgmental way.

Empathy and understanding

Every day, aim to be more empathic. Aim to see people, and think, *What is this person going through?* See someone walking like a tough guy and understand that he may have grown up in an environment that forced him to be this way, where weakness was death. See someone crying over a lost love, and understand that in that moment for that person, this is the worst thing that could happen – even if to others it does not seem so bad. See a dog moping around, looking bored, and understand that the dog is starving for even basic attention, a small caress. See a mother yelling at her kids in the streets for fighting with each other, where she grabs them roughly and drags them with her in a fury. Then, understand that perhaps this is a single mother who has had to take drastic actions to keep control of her children, to keep them out of trouble.

Empathy is finding a point of understanding, not looking for a way to judge every situation. Our internal judge, as it is a powerful force on the world around us, ultimately becomes our own enemy. The judge you inflict on others with your mind is the same one that will judge your own actions harshly later. You will be plagued with bad thoughts about every little thing you do wrong if you do not regain control of that judge. I have found that a daily practice of empathy, of seeking to deeply understand people, even people who seem to come from another world, has helped me to not have to judge. I am free from needing to judge everything as good or bad. It just is, and I can relax and be free in my mind. Learning to be more understanding of ourselves helps to build empathy for others and building empathy for others helps us to be more understanding of ourselves.

Forgiveness

What you can give is forgiveness, which is a greater gift to yourself than anyone else. I aim to forgive and forget everything that has gone wrong in my life. Just remember the lessons that are critical. For the actual wrong or who did it, forget about it. We all make mistakes. *Don't you wish other people would forgive and forget your mistakes?* I don't understand why we must criticize someone for making a mistake, then remember it and criticize him again and again, for a mistake that was made once. If a mistake was made once, go over it one time with the person who made it so that he understands how to fix it, and then move on.

Learn from nature. Does the dog hold on to a mistake, worrying about it? Does the bird? Does the tree? Does the wind?

When something happens that I feel is unjust, I have learned that for most of these minor events it is best to let it go. Getting angry and emotional about small everyday setbacks is not worth it. If you must use your energy on something, save it for a big issue, not for something rather trivial. How do you know the difference? Something trivial will not matter and probably even be forgotten in a week. The consequences for losing your composure or for lashing out are often much greater than if you could simply let it go and move on with your life. Aim to forgive and forget the small things when it comes to people you care about. But if someone is taking advantage of your kindness and good nature, remember their tendencies and just avoid interacting with such people.

New creations – art, music, dance, jokes

As humans, we also have the gift of creativity. Some people say that they are not creative, but we all have this innate ability and sometimes we just need to find the right inspiration. If you do not believe that you are creative, remember that you have many dreams every night, where your brain automatically creates many different scenarios. We are all creative – it's so easy you can do it in your sleep. Some people may be more inclined to create with words, painting, dance, or with building something. But these are all creative forms of expression.

These are gifts that do not need to be given to one particular person. Sometimes, your act of creating allows many, many people to benefit from that. Think of art that ends up in museums, for example. These are single artworks that are given to countless visitors to enjoy. If you would like, you can always turn your own house into a museum of your own artistic creations, for the viewing pleasure of anyone who may visit.

Ideas

I am a big proponent of exercising your "idea muscle" regularly. When you do this, you will find that acquiring new ideas, even great ideas, is not especially difficult. It is a matter of practicing coming up with new ideas on a regular basis. When you reach a point of immense idea generation abilities, you will have more ideas than you know what to do with.

Some people get bright ideas as a matter of routine. If you have an idea that you think could benefit many people, share it. Tell someone who can possibly put it into action. Don't keep it secret, because in time you may forget about it and eventually someone else will put it into action anyway. Most ideas that we think are original are thought up by other people soon enough, or perhaps were already thought up in the past. You might as well give it to someone who can do something with it. Remember that in the fast-paced world that we live in, an idea that is valuable today may become obsolete tomorrow. If your idea is truly valuable and you communicate it to the right person, then that person may want to team up with you to help turn the idea into a reality. In giving away a bright idea, you likely have little to lose, and everything to gain.

If you would like to be able to generate more creative ideas, you may be interested in reading my book, *Idea Hacks: Come up with 10X More Creative Ideas in 1/2 the Time*.

The benefit of the doubt

I aim to give the benefit of the doubt as much as I can. You should aim to give the benefit of the doubt as much as you can – unless of course you are in a situation where you feel unsafe or where there is a great risk. In general, it is much healthier to assume the best in people, rather than to assume that they are always trying to get something from you for nothing. Protect yourself in areas where giving the benefit of the doubt could cause you harm, but otherwise, be open to the possibility that people are being truthful and genuine.

My attitude is often "so what." This is how I have learned to give the benefit of the doubt. Imagine that you have a dollar in your hands, and someone comes up to you and asks for it, because he needs it to help feed his family. Perhaps you can have skeptical thoughts, and think *Well, his shoes are too new, he talks as if he is well educated for someone who is struggling. He looks clean, like he comes from a good home. Maybe he wants it for drugs.* Or, you can think, *I don't know his situation. Perhaps he does need this, and he really does have a family.* When my inner skeptic takes over, I find myself saying "so what." If he chooses to waste the money, then that is not my problem. If he chooses to lie, that is not my problem. If he does indeed plan to use the money for good and if he is telling me the truth, then I want to be there to help him. I don't want to be someone who assumed the worst, and then failed to help someone who was honest and in need.

Think of All the Gifts You Have Received in This Life

What have your parents or your caretakers given you that they were not required to give? For instance, we know that parents must love, feed, clothe, and shelter, but many parents do much more than just this.

If you eat meat, how many animals have "given" their lives for you?

In a time of great need, has anyone ever stopped to notice, and given you something to help?

Have you ever been given a helpful piece of wisdom that you needed at that moment?

Has anyone ever given you something or an opportunity that you knew you had not specifically earned? It was just a gift.

Do people often tell you, you have a gift, a talent that many others do not have?

Were you born healthy? Are you generally healthy now?

Do you have all of your limbs, fingers, and toes?

Appreciate these gifts, and then stop and think, *What can I do to return the favor to the world, for all of these great gifts I have received?*

Life Begins with a Gift

Of all the gifts you have been given, the greatest one would have to be life itself.

You were born because your parents, and ultimately the universe, God, nature, or whichever force you believe in was responsible for giving you this life. Life begins with a gift. If you were ever looking for a philosophical message to guide your life, perhaps the universe itself was trying to tell us something, since we all came into existence through the gift of life. In a loving family, this new life will be the greatest gift that they could ever receive. Interestingly, you do not get to see the joy of your family and just how wonderful of a gift you were to the world. Your infant brain was still forming, and of course you did not process the moments fully, and later you would not recall them. However, you have likely experienced a new family member coming into your life at some point, and you can understand the great joy that this brings.

Expect Less and Give What You Can

Become a self-sustaining person, aiming to give more and to take less. Do not feel bad if you are not at this level yet – this is something to work toward. Of course, there is no problem with asking for some help, but we should do our best to give at least as much as we receive. Ideally, we would give more than we receive.

My father sometimes tells me about what life was like when he was a kid, growing up in a small village in Mexico. My father's father (and my grandfather), Apolonio, was a very hard worker, and he worked his kids on the farm – as was normal for the times. My grandfather took care of himself and his family well enough that they often produced more crops and food than what they needed. And in those times and in that place, you could be viewed as wealthy if your basic survival needs were met and if you had anything extra left over. Sometimes other villagers would come to Apolonio asking if he had some extra crops to spare, and when he did he would always give some away.

My grandfather didn't expect anything from others, and he gave away what he could.

People in society often get upset because they expect someone else to take care of their problems. Instead, we need to rise up, fix some problems for ourselves, and then give some of the surplus away. We can't expect anyone else to save us from our problems. When we rely too heavily on the town, the city, the nation, the government, we forget that *we* are the people who make up these groups. It is us, in our concrete real forms that can make a difference. It is not the abstract idea of a faceless group of people that will change things. *We must do it ourselves.*

Here I am principally referring to people who *can control something*, who *can do something*, who *have resources to do something*, but who still blame others for their own setbacks. As individuals, we all have to learn to do our own part and play our own role. As far as I'm concerned, the government is there to support us when it is functioning well, but they cannot save us.

"Ask not what your country can do for you. Ask what you can do for your country." – John F. Kennedy

This is one of my favorite quotes, but in my mind, I always generalize it further. I turn it into "Ask not what other people can do for you. Ask what you can do for yourself and for other people." In other words, don't sit around waiting for others to give you something. Give it to yourself and give it to others when you can too. If you do not know what your gift is, do not worry. We all have a gift. And here is one gift we are all born with. Your gift and the gift we all have is this: *We are the gift that keeps on giving. We have the gift of the potential for endless giving.*

Still trying to find your gift? Perhaps it hasn't been given to you yet, and you need to give it to yourself. You can do this through learning and building up your skills.

The Power of Giving

As revealed in *Man's Search for Meaning*, the author and psychologist Viktor Frankl recounts his experience as a prisoner in a concentration camp in Nazi Germany. In his time there, he realized that those who had purpose were much more likely to survive than those who were not able to keep a firm purpose in mind. In his case, obviously he wanted to get back to his family and to be free once again, as surely all the prisoners did. But his purpose was also to complete a manuscript which would ultimately recount his experiences as a prisoner, and the importance of finding meaning in life, even when going through immense suffering. He did eventually write the manuscript, which ultimately became *Man's Search for Meaning*, one of the bestselling books of all time. I believe Viktor Frankl realized that as cruel and inhumane as his experience had been, that it all had to be for something. It all had to be for a larger purpose, and that purpose ended up being to teach people the importance of purpose, of finding meaning even in apparently hopeless circumstances. His revelations were a great gift to humanity, and his book is one of the most powerful ones I have ever read.

In *438 Days*, written by Jonathan Franklin, we learn of the incredible story of Salvador Alvarenga who worked in Mexico as a fisherman. Tragically, after a violent storm he found himself stranded at sea in a small boat. As difficult as it may be to imagine, he managed to survive being stranded in the ocean for 438 days. One of his survival techniques was to catch birds that landed on the boat, and he would break one wing so that they could not fly away. This way, he could keep a surplus of food with him. What gave him the strength to keep going for so long, despite a seemingly hopeless situation? He wanted to be a part of his 13-year-old daughter's life, Fatima, who he had not seen since she was a baby. He wanted to be a true father to her. Also, he felt that he was chosen to bring back a message of hope for people to never feel suicidal because he believed that if he could survive this ordeal, then people should be able to overcome anything. He had a deep desire to give – he wanted to give himself fully as a father to his child, and he wanted to give hope to those who were feeling hopeless.

Here I will give an example from my life, which of course I do not intend to compare with the prior examples, but to show you a more everyday sort of example. As a child I was so phobic of public speaking that much of the time, when I had an assignment for class that involved speaking, I would pray for some miracle and for school to be cancelled on the day of my assignment. Of course, I was never so lucky. Sometimes, I would actually feel sick from the anxiety, and I would stay at home, avoiding the assignment in this way.

As I grew up and got older, I still found it very difficult to speak in public. Then, when I was in graduate school, I realized that public speaking was going to be required, and it was going to happen often — for classes, meetings, and conferences. It was clear that I needed to overcome this fear, so I spent some time reflecting on how to resolve my problem. After some reflection, I had discovered what I must do. The solution was actually much simpler than I had imagined. I overcame my phobia by focusing outward on what I was teaching, and how the information would be useful to the audience, rather than on my internal worries of making a fool of myself — or on my general belief that I was a horrible public speaker. I turned the focus to what I could give to others, rather than worrying about what negative judgments I might receive. I filled my mind with an energy for giving, and there was no space left over to worry about whether people would dislike my presentation or think that I was a fool, or anything like that.

The unifying theme here is that when we face the most difficult circumstances, we should turn our focus to what it is that we can give to others. When you focus on what you will be able to give instead of just on what you can take, you will find true strength from within to keep pressing on even through the most difficult of circumstances.

When Not to Give (or Give Rarely)

I want to be perfectly clear, that I do not recommend that *everyone* apply this 7th Thought right away. This Thought is for those who are in a position to give. This is for those who have the time, the energy, and the means to give. Give when your heart is overflowing with a giving energy, and for no other reason.

The following are the cases when you should *not* give, or when you should give rarely.

If you are still working on meeting your own needs, then do not give much. Remember what they tell you when you are on an airplane – to put on your own oxygen mask *first* in the event of an emergency. You must help yourself before you can help others.

If you have met your needs, but you are working a lot for this, so you feel overly stressed, then do not give too much. In that case, you still need to take care of yourself. Don't feel bad about it. Take care of yourself fully and when you are feeling your best, then you will be in a better position to give to others.

If someone is putting pressure on you to give, do not allow them to influence you. Give what you want to give when you want to give. Giving is an expression of love and caring and empathy, and for people to demand that you give, or guilt you into giving is not right for them to do. You do not owe anyone anything. If you do owe, it is called a debt, not a gift. As with my rule about not buying something in the moment if someone is trying to sell me an item, if someone asks me to give them something and it is substantial, then I do not make a choice in the moment. You get to decide what is substantial, and this figure will vary for everyone. Just set your personal limit and stick to it.

Do not ever give or offer any more than you can afford to lose. When someone asks you for a substantial sum of money, keep in mind that you are put in this position. Do not give more money than you would be comfortable with losing. I rarely lend money, but if I do, I treat it as a gift. To me, it's not worth the disappointment of lending money and then the person not wanting to pay it back. I give or I do not give, and I avoid lending.

Lending is a contract – and I prefer contracts only in cases where I truly need them – with some business deals, for example.

If you could be in harm's way or in danger by giving, then do not do it. If you live in a big city, and you are alone at night and a strange person asks you for money, it may be best to politely say "No" and to keep on walking away. Certain situations are not worth the potential harm. This isn't about being negative, it's about taking reasonable actions to keep yourself safe, and not to allow your willingness to give to turn you into a target.

Exercises

Make a list of all of the things you are in a position to give

Consider what we are *all* in a position to give: kindness, love, an ear to listen and *not* judge, empathy and understanding, forgiveness, new creations, and the benefit of the doubt.

Ask yourself: *What can I give today?*

Are you in the position to give some items away? Make a list of them, or better yet, find a box or grab some bags and start putting in items that you are ready to give away. This serves two functions – you can clear out things that you no longer need or perhaps do not want, and you can give them to someone who needs them. I aim to keep others in mind and not just myself when I look for things to give away. For example, recently I was looking through my shoes and I realized that I had an older pair that I don't use anymore. They are still in good enough condition where they would be useful to someone in need. At first, I was tempted to keep them as a backup pair of shoes, but then I realized that this pair would just sit there most likely and go unused. Winter was approaching, and I thought – surely someone needs these shoes much more than I do. I decided to give them away.

After you have gathered your items together, the next step is to find the right agency, community, or person to give your items to. Look online or ask around. I am sure you will quickly find the right people to give your items to.

I want to offer a suggestion if you feel uncomfortable offering your items to someone. You may be embarrassed to ask if someone needs an item and risk offending them. I was recently in this position myself. I was visiting London and I went to a restaurant and ordered far too much food. I didn't have anywhere to save the food for myself, but I wasn't going to throw it away either. I decided to get it in a to-go box, and to look for someone who may need it. There are many homeless people in London, as there are in most big cities. But on this day I had a difficult time finding anyone to give it to. Then I saw someone who looked very worn out, exhausted, pacing back and forth, and seemed to be selling or giving away a newspaper, I wasn't sure which. I had a feeling that he needed the food, but I wasn't sure, and I didn't want to offend him. I thought for a moment, and I came up with a solution. I went up to him with the food, and I said: "Excuse me, I have some leftover food here. *Do you know anyone who could use this?*" He smiled and said yes, and I gave it to him.

Make a list of the most meaningful things (even if it wasn't an actual thing) that you have ever received

We have to understand that the things we receive often are not so important themselves, but sometimes they come to represent something greater. Perhaps you were the best employee at your work, and so your boss rewarded you with an amazing bonus to show that he noticed your hard work and that he appreciated it. You may have been highly stressed at a difficult time, and someone gave you a gift to help brighten your mood – and this made all the difference. Or perhaps you had an unbreakable bond with someone, and this person gave you a gift that touched your soul and showed you just how deeply you were understood. Of course, you may have received highly practical gifts as well – perhaps someone offered you a place to stay when you were unable to pay for it. Or perhaps someone gave you some clothes or silverware, or toys for your children, or other necessary items when you struggled to pay the bills. An alternative gift is to be given the gift of a revelation – someone may have said or done something which allowed you to have a great realization that changed your life. Whatever gift you received, think of how good it felt to receive it, and how important it was for you at that moment.

Send a message to someone, giving thanks for something that this person did

Giving is such a wonderful and heartfelt thing to do, that we should be sure to always encourage this in others. When someone gives you something, be sure to thank this person for it. If this act of giving had some great meaning for you, try to express this in some way to the giver. The act of giving is so powerful that sometimes the person who gives does not comprehend just how important and meaningful this act was.

Create something and give it away

Doing this showcases the most unique parts of yourself, because anything you make will carry your unique creative fingerprint on it. This means no one else would have made something exactly like it, with the purpose that you had. You may consider writing a poem or story, drawing, coloring (e.g., Mandala's are popular), recording yourself singing or dancing or making your own music, building a model car or boat, or making your own card with your own art and message. You may even consider making soaps, jewelry, scarves, or clothing. It is so easy in this era to figure out how to make anything, that there are no excuses to not do it. You may watch videos on YouTube to learn, since you can visually see how something is made, and then try it for yourself. If you prefer to do something as a group, you could do improvisational comedy, or you could create your own short film with friends. Whatever it is, have fun doing it.

With your loved ones, always remember anyone who is going through a difficult time in life

Our loved ones are the most important people in our lives. Keep in mind anyone who is sick or injured or going through a great battle of some kind – perhaps a divorce or overcoming a trauma. When life is going well for us, it is easy to forget that life isn't always good for everyone. Make efforts to build empathy and be aware of what is going on with your loved ones. Many of us, when facing difficult times, do not necessarily open up. We may become guarded and not discuss our troubles openly. Respect people's privacy and their desires, but it helps to let them know that you are there, that you are available to talk or to help. Sometimes the greatest gift is just being available and caring about another person.

The most difficult thing to do is to battle our problems alone. Often, people just want to feel that someone else is there to support them, even if it is in some small way. A simple gesture, like remembering to pick up the phone and call someone who is going through a difficult time, can go a long way.

Elevate Your Life with the *7 Thoughts*

"Carefully watch your thoughts, for they become your words. Manage and watch your words, for they will become your actions. Consider and judge your actions, for they have become your habits. Acknowledge and watch your habits, for they shall become your values. Understand and embrace your values, for they become your destiny."

– Mahatma Gandhi

The Most Important Thoughts to Have

Your Thoughts have immense power to guide your life, and so you must choose carefully what it is that you think about. Start with the *7 Thoughts* of this book:

1. Focus on what you can control, *not* on what you cannot control
2. Focus on the positive, *not* the negative
3. Focus on what you can do, *not* on what you cannot do
4. Focus on what you have, *not* on what you do not have
5. Focus on the present, *not* on the past and future
6. Focus on what you need, *not* on what you want
7. Focus on what you can give, *not* on what you can take

Everything comes from thought. If we can improve the quality of our thoughts, then we can produce words that empower us and enlighten us rather than those that weaken us and make us feel disordered. Through better thinking, we can take actions as a human collective that direct us toward prosperity and freedom, instead of misery and the confinement of our true abilities.

Why do these thoughts matter? In the end, the point of these Thoughts is to allow you to become a limitless being, unshackled by the side of your mind that is destructive, and to unleash the constructive force within you.

The purpose of having these Thoughts in our lives is that they shall help us on our journey to meeting our full potential. When we reach this potential for ourselves, we will be able to touch other lives, and help them to do the same. Eventually, we will all be elevated to exponentially higher and higher levels.

Reaching your potential is about being happy, peaceful, living a life of meaning, living out your purpose, and spreading joy and love and positivity instead of the opposite. This is the point. This is what we are here to do.

Remember this: You have the power to create the world that we were all meant to live in. You alone can spark change.

You Create Your Reality

The Thoughts in this book are not new, but that does not make them any less important. These thoughts were drawn from my personal inspiration, multiple philosophies (from the ancient west to the ancient east), religions, and from modern scientific findings. I have done what I could to identify the 7 most important thoughts that we should have more of to live a good life of happiness, peace, and meaning, and to reduce the needless pain and suffering that we bring upon ourselves and the world. Generally, I wished to help you gain personal freedom from the trivial things in life, and to make the best of whatever situation you may have in front of you.

One way of making the best of your situation is to understand that you are playing an active role in forming your reality. You are not a passive bystander. **There is immense power and energy within your Thoughts to create the life that you want to make for yourself.**

If you are not convinced yet, here is some of the evidence to support this (Note that some of this is a review from prior sections.):

Self-fulfilling prophecy

Whatever it is that you think will happen is probably what will happen. This is because your mind will tend to cause to happen that which you expect to happen. This effect is so powerful that if you think you have been cursed with black magic and you expect to die, you may indeed perish. Also, if you believe you can achieve some immense success that most people would be unable to achieve, simply in your believing this strongly, you will be much more likely to achieve it. I am not saying that thinking about something is enough to make it happen, rather what I am saying is that thoughts influence your biology and actions, and much of the time, *your thoughts become your reality*. And while this effect is quite powerful, of course there are limits.

Growth mindset

The growth mindset theory was proposed by Carol Dweck. The theory says that if you believe you are capable of improving in your abilities, then you will be much more effective in your pursuits, because you will seek opportunities for growth and work hard to achieve your goals. However, if you believe that your abilities are fixed and that you cannot improve them, then you will not be as effective in your pursuits. Your belief that you are limited will mean that you do not seek out many growth or learning opportunities, because you think it won't help you to improve. You will think that you have a set of attributes, and not much can be done to change them. It turns out that both viewpoints are correct, because whichever case you believe in, you are likely to create that reality for yourself. Again, here we see that your thoughts are creating the world around you. Simply believing that you can learn and grow, makes you likely to work hard when needed, which in turn allows you to improve in your abilities.

Placebo effect

This is the effect where you are typically given a sugar pill (without an active ingredient) to treat a medical condition, and you would be told that the pill is medicine – which of course is untrue. As an example, a person with a medical condition will take a placebo pill and then report feeling better afterward, even though it had no medicinal ingredients in it. This effect is discussed in the book *Cure* by Jo Marchant. One interesting insight from the book is that even when a patient is told that she is being given a placebo, the placebo effect still works, showing that deception is not always necessary to obtain the positive effects. Also, it was discussed that the placebo effect is not "all in the mind," where you trick yourself into thinking you are feeling better when really you are not. Rather, the body, upon receiving a signal of healing, the pill, is then capable releasing natural painkilling chemicals which can make a person feel better or heal better. Of course, there are limits to what the body is capable of doing. For instance, if you accidentally cut off your finger, a placebo will not help you to grow it back. This is not magic or supernatural. Science is just beginning to understand the powers of the mind to influence our health.

Confirmation bias

Confirmation bias means that most of us tend to look for evidence that reinforces our currently existing beliefs, and we do not pursue, or we disregard evidence that conflicts with that belief.

Take a moment to think of something that you believe in. For instance, it could be that you have a belief that one political party is better than the other, or that you are highly skilled at something, or that your friend has a specific personality type. The belief could be something you hold deeply, or just something that you have acquired from repeated experience. Think about this carefully – do you tend to only perceive the evidence that already supports your belief? Do you really consider any evidence that conflicts with your belief, or do you tend to forget about it or to assume that those are simply exceptions or even false?

As an example of confirmation bias at work, consider a 7-year-old boy that I was once introduced to. One of the first things he told me was that he knew Spanish. He could tell you the names of the main colors and numbers up to 20 in the language. However, if you actually spoke to him in Spanish, he could not follow the conversation. Since he lived in the US, it was easy for him to focus on the evidence that supported that he was good at Spanish. He knew more than most kids for where he lived, and he knew more than his own parents. This seems like pretty good support that he knew Spanish, but of course, this did not mean that he *truly* knew the language. Most kids in the US do not study it, meaning it does not take much skill to surpass most kids. And his parents did not study the language either. He knew some of the basics of Spanish, but that was all. This seems like a trivial example, but I want you to realize that basically all of us have such mistaken ideas about ourselves – this is because we have confirmation bias.

Our thoughts have a heavy influence on our lives because we tend to look only for ways to confirm what we already believe. This makes us continue to believe what we already believe in, even if the objective evidence does not truly support the belief. Be careful what you think of, because it is hard to change your mind once you think it! Make it a point to look for evidence that could disconfirm your beliefs, which would be competing evidence to what you believe. For example, if you find yourself interrupting someone when you disagree with him, and not letting him speak his mind, learn to stop this habit. Allow others to say what they think and listen with an open mind to it. Consider deeply that their statements may be true, that they may be partly true, or that the perspective may at least come from genuine experiences. You do not need to change your mind and agree with everyone, but when you strongly disagree with someone, force yourself to open up and truly listen – because if you don't, then you are exhibiting confirmation bias.

Are You Going to Heal Us with Your Potion, or Sicken Us with Your Poison?

People focus a lot on what makes us different, and we categorize ourselves based on those differences – we're from different countries and regions, people have different accents, heights, weights, skin tones, bone structures, scents, goals, intellects, incomes, sexual orientations, religious beliefs, political ideologies, educational attainments, and so forth. All these differences seem to distract us from the fact that we're all mostly the same in that we all have needs, desires, hopes, and dreams. Yet I suppose it is human nature that we hyper-focus on our differences.

A very wise person that I know once told me that he believes humans are not independent like we think we are. Instead, we are all very interrelated. He said that we are like the Pando tree in Utah, US– this appears to be a collection of 47,000 independent trees, but in fact is one organism – with an interconnected root system. As a fun fact, the Pando tree is believed to be 80,000 years old and is the heaviest organism on Earth weighing 6 million kilograms. Perhaps humans are not so different than these trees. We are all integral to working together as a whole, whether we can see it or not. Think of the Betterfly and Bitterfly Effects – one person's joy or pain may be felt miles away, or even on the other side of the world.

I will ask you to think of everything you do as potion or poison. *Are you going to heal us with your potion, or sicken us with your poison?* A straightforward way to apply this in your life is to ask yourself when you are about to do something:

What would the result be if everyone did what I am about to do? Would this make our lives better as a whole, or would it make them worse?

We are all part of one root system, so what heals one heals many, and what poisons one poisons many.

Our challenge is to learn to love ourselves, then others, then nature, then the earth, then the universe and everything as it happens. If we love and forgive ourselves then we should love and forgive all because no single one of us is better than the rest of us. We are all the same, but we will not realize this unless we are able to look beyond our superficial features.

From Weakness to Strength

Do you feel weak?

The more suffering and dilemma's you have gone through in your life, the more of a position you are in to truly make a difference in this world. Those who feel weakest are often at the cusp of doing the bravest thing they've ever done in their whole life. People who feel like they are battered and about to be broken, are instead about to reveal to the world that they were ultimately unbreakable.

It is those who feel the most powerless, lost, lonely, and forgotten who have the greatest capacity and strength inside. They have faced down a dark void inside of them, and they have come out alive when they thought it would eat them alive. They have battled the most powerful enemy there is – the human mind, and they have begun to conquer it, which means they can begin to conquer their dreams, whichever ones they shall set their hearts on. I have seen people feeling their weakest, their most brittle, ready to fail, ready to give up and die. Then, they found one last bit of inner strength that turned everything around and transformed their whole reality. I have done this myself, I have seen it in others, and I believe we are all capable of doing this. At some point, we all have to face this ultimate test of who we are.

We must use all our strengths to overcome our inherently destructive minds, to forge a constructive, creative, loving reality that endures. We are all independent, but we are all together in this (e.g., like the Pando tree with interconnected roots). Do what's best for you but do it in a way that is good for everyone.

In times of weakness, remember love. When you are at your lowest lows and empty and drained and in a negative state, remember love. Remember the love of your parents, of siblings, of great friends. Remember its power and seek not just to receive it but to give it as well. Love is all-important. Those who lose love become lost and everything loses meaning. If you are not doing something to help people that you love, to bring them joy and to ease their sufferings then everything starts to seem meaningless. Love is an energy, it is like a glue that holds societies together. The more we love, the more we can accomplish together. Give love to the people you care about and to yourself as well.

The Daily Practice

"If we could change ourselves, the tendencies in the world would also change. As a man changes his own nature, so does the attitude of the world change towards him.... We need not wait to see what others do."
– Mahatma Gandhi

Whatever it is that you practice in your life is what you are becoming. Figure out what it is that you want to become, and practice that every day. Understand that whatever you practice every day, you will bring out in the world.

If you want to live in a disciplined world, practice discipline every day.

If you want to live in a giving world, practice giving every day.

If you want to live in a considerate world, practice consideration every day.

If you want to live in a patient world, practice patience every day.

If you want to live in a beautiful world, practice artistic expression every day.

If you want to live in a peaceful world, practice peace every day.

If you want to live in a healthy world, eat well, exercise, and think good thoughts every day.

Practice it with every fiber of your being, with everything you are.

This is called a practice because it is not always automatic. You must consciously choose your thoughts and actions, and not expect them to happen without effort.

Conversely, if you do not want to live in an undisciplined, ungiving, inconsiderate, impatient, ugly, unpeaceful, unhealthy world, then do not practice such things every day.

Understand that just by being you and knowing what you stand for and knowing what you believe in, you are able to shape the world into being what you think it should be. The effects are not immediate. This is not magic. It will take time and you will need to be patient. You will find that with maintaining your daily practice, day after day, year after year, you will affect one life, then two, then three, then those lives will affect other lives, creating a multiplier effect. Then, when you affect ten lives, you are really affecting a hundred, because those ten are each effecting ten more. Eventually, your thoughts and actions are felt on the other side of the world.

Measure your progress not just by what you practice, but measure it by these questions:

What did I practice today that puts me on the right path, no matter how difficult it was to do?

What did I resist today that would have put me on the wrong path, no matter how difficult it was to resist?

Remember this: Whatever it is that you want the world to be, practice it *yourself* every day. We cannot ask of the world what we ourselves are unwilling to do.

How to Make the Best Use of the 7 Thoughts

This book is not a theoretical exercise. I do not want anyone to read it and then put it away and forget about it. The Thoughts must be applied, or they are worthless. The Thoughts must be put into Action, or they are pointless. Thoughts stuck in the mind are like lightning bugs trapped in a bottle. They are not going anywhere. Set your Thoughts free to light up the world and make a difference. I want you to make the best use of the *7 Thoughts to Live Your Life By*, so here are some tips to help.

Find a partner to help elevate each other to higher and higher levels

Often, when we decide to make a change for ourselves, this is a big struggle. We tend to have habits that we have had for many years if not decades, and to change anything becomes a great challenge. If you are committed to adopting the *7 Thoughts* in your life and to changing your focus, I would recommend that you find someone who can give you encouragement, and you can also encourage this person in return. Any time that you struggle with a Thought, or any time that you struggle to find the best path forward with a problem in your life, you can help each other with this. A key point is that you should *both* be there for each other in your struggles. This is a give and take from both sides, not just give, not just take. When you help to elevate your partner to a higher level, you elevate yourself as well.

Here are some benefits to having a partner. Any time you help your partner, you learn something new and better your own life as well. Also, you can commit to pointing out weak areas in each other without judgment, as this is typically something that is difficult for family and friends to discuss, since they do not want to hurt your feelings. Another benefit is that people who partner up tend to meet their goals more quickly and reliably – whether it is to be happier, more successful, or to focus more on the important things in life. Lastly, this is a good way to form a lifelong bond with someone, which is not an easy thing to do. I do not recommend that you automatically go to a friend – make sure to find a partner who is ready to help and be helped so that you can both grow together.

You may already have someone in mind. If not, you could look on social media and post something such as: "I am looking for a partner to apply the *7 Thoughts to Live Your Life By*. Who is ready to join me in transforming our lives, one Thought at a time?"

Affirmations

Affirmations are statements or commands that we repeat to ourselves, and where we focus intently on a message that we want to make a reality. It helps if we visualize ourselves acting out or living out the affirmation. Some people seem to think that affirmations have a magical quality, as if you wish for something, and then simply stating it out loud makes it happen. Of course, this is not what is happening. What having affirmations does is it proves to yourself that this is something truly important in your life that you are committed to. You are thinking about it, saying it, visualizing it, and likely then forming a plan for how to accomplish it. Your conscious and subconscious mind then become linked together for a common purpose, allowing you to increase the chance of making your affirmations come true.

Many people just think: *Sure, I should work harder to be successful, I get it.* But the thought itself is unconvincing, and it passes through them rapidly and then they proceed to waste their time, life, and energy. They have not given themselves a powerful message or affirmation, and they have not committed their full attention to it. Rather, people who form affirmations tend to be more specific, positive, and have a more powerful drive when they frame their desires, thus making them much more likely to convert their dreams into a reality.

Many famous and influential people have used affirmations in their lives, such as: Oprah Winfrey, Jim Carrey, Denzel Washington, and Jennifer Lopez to name a few. Consider using the *7 Thoughts* as affirmations until you internalize them, and you no longer need to repeat and visualize them to yourself because you embody the Thoughts, living them out every day.

If you would like to use the *7 Thoughts* as affirmations, I recommend rephrasing them in this way:

1. **I will focus on what I *can* control, not on what I *cannot* control**
2. **I will focus on the positive, *not* the negative**
3. **I will focus on what I can do, *not* on what I *cannot* do**
4. **I will focus on what I have, *not* on what I *do not* have**
5. **I will focus on the present, *not* on the past and future**
6. **I will focus on what I need, *not* on what I want**
7. **I will focus on what I can give, *not* on what I can take**

You may repeat these to yourself every morning, or every night, or whenever you wish.

Master One Thought at a Time, and in Order

Remember that when your mind is everywhere, it is nowhere. Now that you are almost finished reading the book, I recommend that you go back and focus more carefully on one Thought at a time. Go in order. There is a logic and flow to how the Thoughts are listed. If you jump straight to the last Thought, focusing on what you can give without having mastered any of the other Thoughts, you are likely to create more problems for yourself. If you focus on the third Thought, paying more attention to what you can do before you have taken the time to consider the first thought, what you can control, then you will be overwhelmed with options, likely unable to make progress.

Spend as much time as you need on each Thought. Remember to perform the exercises at the end of each section – I included them because I thought they would truly help you. Refer to them often so that you can develop a daily practice, implementing the 7 Thoughts in your life day by day through your actions. This is crucial, so I will repeat it here in other words.

Breathe life into the Thoughts through your Actions. Those Actions will become Habits that have the Power to Transform your Life.

Do not be in a rush, as this is not a contest. To obtain full mastery of every Thought, you must put your full focus, time, and attention on each one.

Are You Ready to Awaken?

When you have understood the 7 Thoughts fully with your Mind, Body, Heart, and Soul, you will be ready to receive the greatest gift that I can give you.

This is the gift of an *Awakening*.

The awakened spirit will be able to:

- Consciously use the *7 Thoughts* to create a good, happy, peaceful, and meaningful life
- Understand that a simple Thought holds immense power, and can have effects on the other side of the world
- Develop a higher level of control over the mind – to stay positive and calm even during negative and chaotic circumstances
- Let go of the need to control everything, and especially to let go of the need to control those things which were never controllable
- Be a great source of positive energy, and diminish or stop creating experiences of sorrow, anxiety, stress, and pain for oneself and for others
- Turn a Superpain into a Superpower, meaning to convert painful, difficult, or negative experiences into superpowers, or positive and desirable experiences
- Use the power of the mind to generate solutions rather than to generate problems
- Stop desiring things that serve no greater need or purpose, and which may ultimately serve as distractions from what truly matters
- Accept the Now, love the Now, and understand that the Now is all there is, rather than needing things to be some other way
- Realize that just as necessity is the mother of invention, necessity is the mother of all things that ultimately get done – what you need is what you will get
- Discover one's own gift in order to give it away to the world
- Understand the state of humanity and even of the world, yet not need to judge it all as good or bad

- Use time, life, and energy in a resourceful, creative, positive way, rather than in a wasteful, negative, and destructive way
- Align one's thoughts, words, actions, beliefs, values, and desires to become a unified, happy, and transcendent being

A Note on Mental Health

The 7 Thoughts to Live Your Life By does not claim to be able to help people who have mental health issues. Just because the Thoughts in this book helped me out of my own personal problems does not mean that I think they will be sufficient for everyone. Someone with deep mental health issues will likely need professional help.

As you have seen in this book, I chose to openly discuss my own mental health issues that I battled with. In time, I have learned that we need to be more open about these *quiet battles* that many of us are suffering through. For the people I know who have openly discussed their mental battles, I have come to have a great respect for them.

They are often quiet battles because they happen in the mind, and those who suffer may not want to discuss them openly. This is because they do not want to burden others, to appear weak, or to admit to themselves that they are suffering. They do not want to receive judgments from others. They do not want to explain their illness – and may not be able to explain it. They do not want sympathy or anyone to look down on them. There are many things they do not want, and so they suffer in silence as they fight their own quiet battles – because they don't know what else to do.

We need to learn to discuss such issues more openly. We do not all need to learn to fulfill the role of therapist – leave that to the therapist. However, we should all learn to be more open in accepting people as they are, with all the good and bad that they bring, and with all the beauty and ugliness. Denzel Washington has said: "You pray for rain, you gotta deal with the mud too. That's a part of it." If we are going to enjoy someone's company when they are at their best, we should learn to accept, console, listen, withhold judgment, and help when they are at their worst.

One of my key mistakes when I battled my depression was to want to shut off the pain too much. I would seek to shut off the painful thoughts and become blocked to them. Sometimes I couldn't properly think about the source of the pain *because* I had blocked it. We need to learn to process the pain without always needing to block it. Then, we could examine it and talk about it, so that we could work through it and overcome it. If we block the pain, then it doesn't go away. In seeing it and realizing exactly what it is, it will eventually pass through us and we can move beyond it. I would encourage you to be more open to yourself about how you are feeling and about what is going on in your life. Feel fully what is happening, whether good or bad. Awareness of a problem is the first step to fixing it. If you block the pain too quickly and shut down, then you are not building awareness, you are losing awareness and will be unable to resolve your problems.

If you are suffering from a mental health issue that is getting worse, where you have lost control of your mind, where performing at your best is no longer possible from day to day, I would urge you to get help. Talk to someone you trust, make an appointment with your doctor, talk to a therapist, or call a mental health hotline. Do them all if you must. Whatever you do, do not go through this alone, do not keep it a secret, it is not something to be scared or ashamed of. It is a disorder that has happened to you, as a manifestation of the disorders of society at large. You are not alone in having caused this. We are all in it together.

An important message: If you are thinking of hurting yourself or someone else, drop what you are doing and get help *right now.* **Talk to a doctor or mental health professional** *immediately.*

Understand that even if you have suffered a mental breakdown, then this is not the worst thing that could happen. Think of it like the sunset and the sunrise. The sun comes down and it comes back the following day, brighter than ever. The mind that breaks down can also come back, to have a spectacular breakthrough, stronger than ever.

Perhaps you feel that you do not know anyone with mental health issues, and this is something that does not appear to affect your life. If so, consider yourself blessed. You are probably not suffering through it if you have such thoughts. However, if you think you do not know anyone with a mental health issue, you are most likely wrong. Mental health issues are most certainly affecting someone you know, likely even at this moment.

Here are some important statistics from the National Alliance on Mental Illness (NAMI):

- Approximately 1 in 5 adults in the U.S.—43.8 million, or 18.5%—experiences mental illness in a given year.
- Approximately 1 in 25 adults in the U.S.—9.8 million, or 4.0%—experiences a serious mental illness in a given year that substantially interferes with or limits one or more major life activities.
- Approximately 1 in 5 youth aged 13–18 (21.4%) experiences a severe mental disorder at some point during their life. For children aged 8–15, the estimate is 13%.

What can you do to help someone who may have a mental health issue?

Listen. Do not make it about yourself. Be available. Do not judge. Be open. Acknowledge a person's pain. Be present fully with your emotional and spiritual side, not just your rational side as you talk with this person. You may also recommend the following: exercise, mindfulness and meditation, yoga, to see a doctor or therapist, or to read *7 Thoughts to Live Your Life By*. These are just a few ideas.

Let's Change a Life Together

Do you believe this book could change a life?

Perhaps you have found this book to be life-changing and you can see that it could have this effect on someone else. As you read, you may have been thinking of someone in need, perhaps of someone who lacks direction and support. You may have tried to help this person, but not known what to say or do. Perhaps *7 Thoughts to Live Your Life By* can help.

I believe seemingly small things can change everything around in our lives – it could be a book, a phrase, a hug, a touch, a smile, a moment, or even a Thought. Do not discount the life-changing powers of any of these.

If there is someone you can think of whose life could be greatly impacted by this book, please gift them a copy.

You may give the book away for a birthday or for Christmas, but also keep in mind that an unexpected gift at an unexpected time is usually a welcome surprise as well.

Often, we may recommend a book or a movie or a brand of clothing. There are so many recommendations and advertisements floating around that we can't blame people for failing to act on our recommendations. The best thing to do when you sense that someone you love and care for could truly benefit from something, *is to give it to them*. Understand that the people who need this book the most are unlikely to realize just how much they needed it until they actually have it in their hands.

As the author, I put all of my *Mind-Body-Spirit energy* into this book. I have given all that I could. I have inserted *everything meaningful* that I have learned from having been a deep observer of humankind since I was a child, from deep insights achieved through meditation, from having read over 300 books (with a sizeable portion in self-development, psychology, and philosophy), from my master's degree in psychology, from the life-changing lessons learned through dealing with major depression, and from the deep wisdom which I have absorbed from my parents, brother, wife, extended family, friends, and many more.

This book is Me in book form, as much as is possible. It houses everything I have known and experienced in some form. I hope that it changes your life, and that in changing your life, it changes many more.

If you think this book could touch a life and change it, please give away a copy of it. I would be eternally grateful.

Thank You

Thank you for taking the time to read *7 Thoughts to Live Your Life By*. I hope that you found the information useful. Just remember that a key part of the learning process is putting what you read into practice.

Before you go, I want to invite you to pick up your free copy of *Step Up Your Learning: Free Tools to Learn Almost Anything*. All you have to do is type this link into your browser:

http://mentalmax.net/EN

Also, if you have any questions, comments, or feedback about this book, you can send me a message and I'll get back to you as soon as possible. Please put the title of the book you are commenting on in the subject line. My email address is:

ic.robledo@mentalmax.net

Did You Learn Something New?

If you found value in this book, please review it on Amazon so I can stay focused on writing more great books. Even a short one or two sentences would be helpful.

To go directly to the review page, you may type this into your web browser:

https://mentalmax.net/7Trev

An Invitation to the "Master Your Mind" Community (on Facebook)

I founded a community where we can share advice or tips on our journey to mastering the mind. Whether you want to think more positively, be a better learner, improve your creativity, get focused, or work on other such goals, this will be a place to find helpful information and a supportive network. I hope you join us and commit to taking your mind to a higher level.

To go directly to the page to join the community, you may type this into your web browser:

https://mentalmax.net/FB

More Books by I. C. Robledo

Smart Life Book Bundle (Books 1-6)

The Intellectual Toolkit of Geniuses

Master Your Focus

The Smart Habit Guide

No One Ever Taught Me How to Learn

55 Smart Apps to Level Up Your Brain

Ready, Set, Change

The Secret Principles of Genius

Idea Hacks

Practical Memory

To see the full list of authored books, visit:

https://mentalmax.net/AMZbks